Complete
First Certificate
Workbook *with answers*
Barbara Thomas and Amanda Thomas

CAMBRIDGE
UNIVERSITY PRESS

CAMBRIDGE UNIVERSITY PRESS
Cambridge, New York, Melbourne, Madrid, Cape Town, Singapore, São Paulo, Delhi

Cambridge University Press
The Edinburgh Building, Cambridge CB2 8RU, UK

www.cambridge.org
Information on this title: www.cambridge.org/9780521698320

First published 2008

Printed in the United Kingdom at the University Press, Cambridge

A catalogue record for this publication is available from the British Library

ISBN 978-0-521-69825-2 Student's Book with CD-ROM
ISBN 978-0-521-69826-9 Student's Book with answers and CD-ROM
ISBN 978-0-521-69828-3 Teacher's Book
ISBN 978-0-521-69830-6 Class Audio CDs (3)
ISBN 978-0-521-69827-6 Student's Book Pack
ISBN 978-0-521-69831-3 Workbook with Audio CD
ISBN 978-0-521-69832-0 Workbook with answers and Audio CD

Contents

Unit 1 A family affair

Grammar

Present simple and continuous, present perfect simple and continuous

❶ Read this email and put the verbs in brackets into the correct tense (present simple or continuous, present perfect simple or continuous).

To: Steph

Hi Steph

How are you? I (1) ......*'m having*...................... (have) a lovely time here in Spain. Sorry I (2) ....
(not write) to you for ages but I (3) .... (work) hard here in Spain since I arrived six weeks ago.
I (4) .... (stay) with a lovely family (see photo!) who (5) .... (live)
in a village near Ronda. I (6) .... (think) you'd like it here. The parents are called Diego
(he's a doctor) and Elena. Diego's family (7) .... (always live) here so everybody
(8) .... (know) them. My job is to look after their three children who are 5, 8 and 13.
I (9) .... (get up) every morning at about 6.30 as school (10) .... (start)
early here but then I'm free till they get home at 2.30. I'm supposed to work on Saturdays but if Diego and Elena are here they
often (11) .... (give) me the day off. They (12) .... (go) to Madrid
this weekend so I (13) .... (look after) the children. They (14) .... (play)
in the garden since breakfast though and they're quite happy so I (15) .... (write) emails
all morning. I (16) .... (send) six so far! The two younger children are very sweet but the teenager
(17) .... (always complain) about something. I (18) .... (remember)
being like that though when I was 13.
I won't see you until the end of September because I (19) .... (change) my flight.
I (20) .... (want) to travel round Spain before I come home.

Write back and tell me your news.

Love Emily

Asking questions (present simple)

❷ A week later, Stephanie phones Emily and asks her some questions. Use the prompts to write her questions in the speech balloons.

1 you ever go / seaside?

> *Do you ever go to the seaside?* ....

2 children / speak English?

> ....

3 you like / food?

> ....

4 Diego and Elena / often go away?

> ....

5 What / the family / usually do / Sundays?

> ....

6 Where / Elena / work?

> ....

Vocabulary

Collocations with *make* and *do*

❶ Choose words from the box to make expressions with *make* and *do*. Write them in the correct circle.

an appointment   your best   a course
a decision   homework   a full-time job   a meal
a mess   a noise   a phone call   a photocopy
a promise   the shopping   a sport   the washing-up

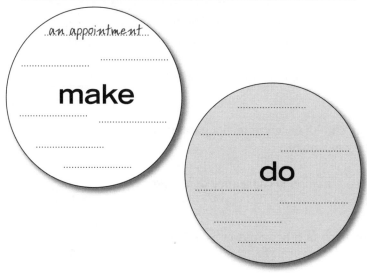

..an appointment..

make

do

❷ Choose one expression to finish each of the sentences below. Write it in the space.

1 Don't worry about the exam. You can only
   do your best .

2 Carla dropped a whole bottle of olive oil and it
   .

3 Everyone was asleep when I came home so I tried
   not to .

4 I wanted to teach art but I didn't have
   the right qualifications so I decided to
   .

5 I needed to have my hair cut so I rang to
   .

6 The fridge was empty because I'd forgotten to
   .

7 Mark didn't want to send the original document
   so he .

8 The sink was full of dirty dishes so I
   .

9 I only have a week's holiday and there are
   so many places I want to go, it's difficult to
   .

10 We were all hungry so Andrea offered to
   .

Phrasal verbs with *make*

❸ Replace the underlined words with one of the phrasal verbs below. You can use one of them twice.

make for   make out   make up

I'd arranged to meet my friend, Tom, in a café. I'd been waiting for him there all evening and I **(1)** was moving towards ....was making for.... the door when I thought I saw him on the other side of the road. I could just **(2)** manage to see .... his black curly hair and the funny scarf he always wears. He was hurrying in the other direction. I ran over to him and he **(3)** invented .... a story about an emergency. We're always arguing. In fact we'd only just **(4)** become friends again .... after our last big argument.

Writing

Spelling and punctuation

Read part of a student's composition and correct the spelling and punctuation. There are 15 mistakes. The first one is corrected for you.

definitely
I ~~definately~~ think that teenage year's should be the best in everyones life because you can have fun and you have fewer problems than adults teenagers know how to have a good time. Most teenagers have a lot of freinds and they discuss things that they are interested in. Teenagers have to be in fashion wearing up-to-date cloths and listening to modern music. They also like to do sports and compete in matchs. But teenager's parents sometimes have a difficult time and they dont understand why? Wouldnt you feel angry if someone went into your room without permission. So do teenagers. As teenagers grow up they stop thinking like children and their believes and their interests change. My opinion is that teenage years are magical and Id like to stay a teenager forever.

Listening Part 3

🎧 **You will hear five different teenagers talking about a family day out. For questions 1–5, choose from the list A–F what each speaker says about the day. Use the letters only once. There is one extra letter which you do not need to use.**

A I was disappointed about something.

B I enjoyed the day more than I had expected.

C I had a better time than some members of my family.

D I was annoyed about a change of plan.

E There wasn't time to do everything I wanted.

F I was relieved that the day was a success.

Speaker 1 [1]

Speaker 2 [2]

Speaker 3 [3]

Speaker 4 [4]

Speaker 5 [5]

Reading Part 3

You are going to read a newspaper article about people who have no brothers or sisters. For questions 1–15, choose from the people (A–E). The people may be chosen more than once.

Which person

realises that the positive relationship they had with their parents is something that not all only children have? **1**

thinks people make a judgement about only children which is mistaken? **2**

thinks being an only child has determined a particular characteristic of their personality? **3**

says they accept their situation because they don't know anything different? **4**

realises that the company of other children is important for only children? **5**

finds their present circumstances a challenge? **6**

says that only children have needs which can be difficult for others to deal with? **7**

realised at a particular point that they were happy being an only child? **8**

was unaware that their reactions to being an only child were not unique? **9**

had problems as a child because they lacked a necessary skill? **10**

has the opinion that there are more disadvantages than advantages? **11**

enjoys having space that is their own? **12**

thinks they developed a better understanding of adults because of being an only child? **13**

mentions a positive benefit of spending a lot of time alone? **14**

is aware that other people feel sorry for them? **15**

Being an only child

"What's it like to spend a lifetime without brothers and sisters?" asks Joanna Moorhead.

A Sam Thompson, aged 10

When my mum's friend had a baby it made me think about being an only child for the first time. I thought, would I like to have brothers and sisters? But to be honest, my friend's sister looked quite annoying – he was always having to watch her and I decided I was better off on my own. There are lots of good things about being an only child. I have privacy, and I like that; some of my friends have to share a bedroom and I know that will never happen to me. Plus I get time on my own with Mum and Dad, and that's special.

One thing that is good is that my friend Thomas lives really close by, so it's easy for me to go and see him. I'd be happy to have just one child, but I'd always make sure we lived close to other kids.

B Bethany Shaw, aged 15

One of the bad things about being an only child when you're young is the reaction you get from other people. They think you're spoilt — you see that look in their eyes. And then you have to prove you're not spoilt, although you know you're not and nor are most only children.

When I was little my friends thought I was lucky being an only one, but now when I tell friends I can tell they're thinking, that must be hard … she's not got a sister to go shopping with, or a brother to help with her homework. All my friends have brothers and sisters and it can be a bit lonely. In general, I think the negatives outweigh the positives, but on the other hand it's all I've known and I'm OK with it.

C Leah Mitchell, aged 29

I went away to school when I was seven, and the hardest thing I found was making friends. Because I was an only child, I just didn't know how to do it. The thing is that when you're an only child you're often the only child in a gathering of adults. I found being an only child interesting, in that it gave me a place at the grown-ups' table and gave me a view into their world that children in a big family might not get. And I know it has, at least partly, made me into the person I am: I never like the idea of being one of a group, for example. I'm not comfortable with being one of a gang.

D Laura Arnold, aged 36

I was a happy child; I had the undivided love and attention of two people, and it made me very confident and secure. I know some only children feel stifled by their parents' constant demands and worries, but that wasn't my experience. I found being an only child enriching, which I think is mainly because we get on so well. I've got two children now and I do find that scary. The problem is I've absolutely no experience of this kind of situation; nothing in my past has prepared me for having to divide myself between the needs of these two little people, and the guilt is hard when I feel I've not been there enough for one of them. And on a practical level, things like sibling rivalry are going to be a whole new ball game.

E Jasmine Weller, aged 49

I always felt a little odd, and assumed it was something about me. It was only in my 30s, when I was training to be a psychotherapist, that I found myself with a group of only children, describing our experiences. It was a revelation because it made me realise that other people felt many of the same things. Growing up in a small unit means we need time to ourselves, which can cause problems with partners and friends, who might misinterpret it as rejection. There are pluses too. Being on your own helps you to become resourceful, and develop your imagination and creativity.

Unit 2 Leisure and pleasure

Grammar

Comparison of adjectives and adverbs

❶ Complete the table with adjectives, adverbs and comparative forms.

Adjective	Comparative form	Adverb
careful		
	easier	
healthy		
fast		
		well
terrible		
		successfully

❷ Fill in the gaps with one of the words from the table.

1 I think eating ...*healthily*... is really important if you want to keep fit.
2 The most .... people I know work incredibly hard.
3 If you had ridden your bike more .... , you wouldn't have had an accident.
4 Learning to play the piano is much .... than I thought.
5 He doesn't play chess as .... as his brother.
6 He dances .... so I couldn't wait for the music to stop.
7 If you keep practising, you'll get ....
8 You need to be more .... when you make your chess moves.

❸ Some of these sentences contain mistakes. Correct the mistakes you find and put a tick (✓) next to the sentences which are correct.

1 Practising every day is the ~~better~~ *best* way to learn an instrument.
2 Golf is the least enjoyable sport to watch on TV. ✓
3 Tennis is the more hardest sport to learn.
4 Riding a motorbike is more fun than taking the bus!
5 It's less easier to learn a new sport as you get older.
6 For me, playing computer games is the more relaxing way to spend my free time.
7 Joining a sports club can help people to become more healthier.
8 I am the fittest now than I have ever been in my life.

✗ Writing

Organising ideas into paragraphs

Look at the task and a student's plan on page 9. Match the selected sentences (1–9) from a student's answer to the correct paragraph (A–D).

1 My sister and I often talk about playing 'Pom Pom Home' and we laugh about all the places we used to hide.
2 I would like to teach this game to my children.
3 It was really exciting when you were able to rescue all your friends.
4 Any number of people can play but it's more fun with between six and eight players.
5 From the ages of about nine to twelve, my favourite game was called 'Pom Pom Home'.
6 On long summer evenings we'd play for hours and come home completely exhausted.
7 To rescue someone you had to run and touch 'home' before the person who was 'IT'.

8   It's basically a more complicated form of 'Hide and Seek', which involves taking people prisoner.

9   I was always really thrilled when my older brother played with us because he was a fast runner and he would always rescue me if I got caught.

This month's writing competition: Children's games

What was your favourite game when you were a child?

Tell us:
- How to play the game
- Why you enjoyed it

The winning article will be published next month.

Student's plan

A   Paragraph 1: Introduction – a brief description of the game and when you played it

Sentences ....5............ ....

B   Paragraph 2: How to play the game

Sentences ....

C   Paragraph 3: Why you enjoyed it

Sentences ....

D   Paragraph 4: Conclusion – your feelings now about the game

Sentences ....

Vocabulary
Adjectives with *-ed* and *-ing*

❶ ⓐ Unjumble the adjectives and write them in the correct sentence.

| irreowd   insoaipdtep   zamigna |
| rsbsraganeim   dihrtlle |

1   He's an .... person; he's not afraid to do anything.

2   I'm really .... Thank you so much. It's what I've always wanted.

3   He should have been here an hour ago. I'm getting ....

4   It was really .... I burnt all the sausages when my friends came over for a barbecue.

5   I was quite .... not to win the tennis match, after I'd trained so hard.

ⓑ Can you think of any other adjectives that would fit in these sentences?

Example
1   a brave person, an incredible person

Phrasal verbs with *off*

❷ Match the phrasal verbs with their definitions.

1	head off	A	start a journey
2	put off	B	leave in a hurry
3	let someone off	C	excuse someone from doing something
4	shoot off	D	interrupt a power supply
5	set off	E	postpone
6	cut off	F	go somewhere

❸ Write one of the phrasal verbs in the correct form in each sentence.

1   We cycled to the swimming pool but it was closed so we *headed off* to the park instead.

2   As soon as they heard the police siren, the burglars .... in their waiting car.

3   They had a long walk ahead of them so they .... down the mountain early in the morning.

4   The lights are not working. I think the electricity has been ....

5   I didn't have to do the test again because the teacher ....

6   The match was .... until the next day because of the rain.

❹ Which of these things can you *take up*, *start up* and *make up*? Put the words under the correct phrasal verb.

a hobby   a machine   an idea   a business   a story   a sport   an excuse

take up	start up	make up
a hobby		

Listening Part 4

Exam information

In Listening Part 4, there are seven questions and you choose one answer from three possible options. You hear the recording twice.

🎧 **You will hear part of a radio interview with Toby Lucas, a young chess player. For questions 1–7, choose the best answer (A, B or C).**

1 Toby joined his chess club because
   A he wanted to play in tournaments with a successful team.
   B he knew there were a lot of good players there.
   C he wanted to meet players of his own age.

2 How useful was playing chess on the internet for Toby?
   A very useful
   B quite useful
   C not at all useful

3 What does Toby like about his favourite grand master?
   A He takes risks.
   B He doesn't mind losing.
   C He always stays calm.

4 When deciding which move to make, Toby usually chooses
   A the one that feels right.
   B an aggressive move.
   C one that he planned before the game.

5 What does Toby say about becoming a top professional player?
   A He needs to work very hard to succeed as a professional.
   B He would enjoy playing professionally.
   C He thinks he lacks the necessary qualities to be a professional.

6 Playing chess has taught Toby to
   A be a more confident person.
   B understand people better.
   C control his body language.

7 According to Toby, how is life different to chess?
   A In chess it is easier to predict what will happen next.
   B You don't need to plan life ahead as much.
   C In chess you have more choices.

Use of English Part 4

For questions 1–8, complete the second sentence so that it has a similar meaning to the first sentence, using the word given. Do not change the word given. You must use between two to five words, including the word given. Here is an example (0).

Example

0 His sister plays chess better than he does.

   AS

   He doesn't play chess ....*as well as*........ his sister.

1 I was really excited during the race because I knew I was going to come first.

   FOUND

   I .... because I knew I was going to come first.

2 The ticket was cheaper than I had expected.

   AS

   The ticket .... I had expected.

3 Eliza was disappointed not to be chosen for the team.

   FOR

   It .... Eliza not to be chosen for the team.

4 The most enjoyable part of the day for Lucy was swimming in the river.

   WHAT

   Swimming in the river .... most about the day.

5 Taking regular exercise is how my grandmother lived to be 100.

   BECAUSE

   My grandmother lived to be 100 .... regular exercise.

6 She prefers tennis to hockey.

   MUCH

   She doesn't .... as tennis.

7 I think golf is more boring than any other sport.

   LEAST

   I think golf .... sport.

8 He plays chess with such confidence that everyone expects him to win.

   CONFIDENT

   He is .... that everyone expects him to win.

Use of English Part 2

For questions 1–12, read the text below and think of the word which best fits each gap. Use only one word in each gap. There is an example at the beginning (0).

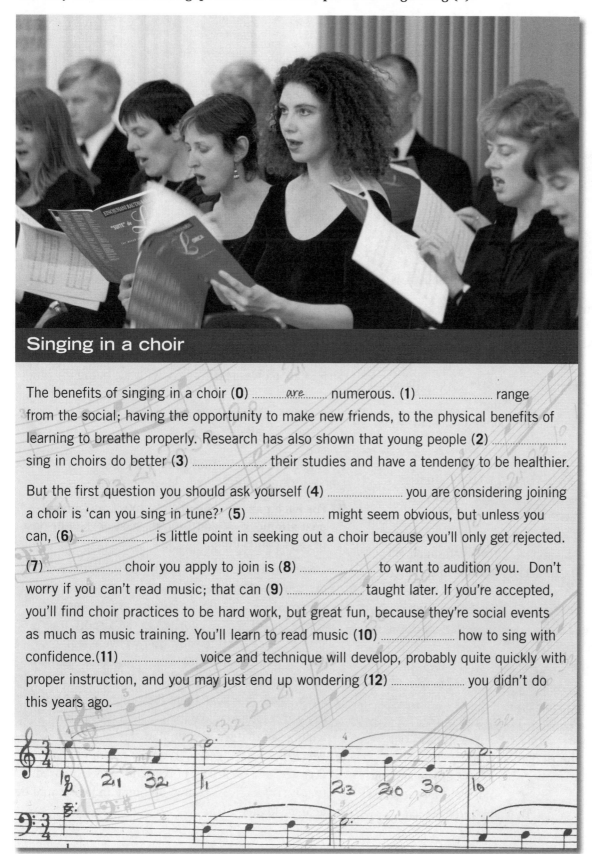

Singing in a choir

The benefits of singing in a choir (**0**) ....*are*.......... numerous. (**1**) .... range from the social; having the opportunity to make new friends, to the physical benefits of learning to breathe properly. Research has also shown that young people (**2**) .... sing in choirs do better (**3**) .... their studies and have a tendency to be healthier.

But the first question you should ask yourself (**4**) .... you are considering joining a choir is 'can you sing in tune?' (**5**) .... might seem obvious, but unless you can, (**6**) .... is little point in seeking out a choir because you'll only get rejected.

(**7**) .... choir you apply to join is (**8**) .... to want to audition you. Don't worry if you can't read music; that can (**9**) .... taught later. If you're accepted, you'll find choir practices to be hard work, but great fun, because they're social events as much as music training. You'll learn to read music (**10**) .... how to sing with confidence. (**11**) .... voice and technique will develop, probably quite quickly with proper instruction, and you may just end up wondering (**12**) .... you didn't do this years ago.

Unit 3 Happy holidays!

Grammar

Past simple and past continuous

❶ **Read these sentences about an overnight train journey from London to Switzerland and put the verbs in brackets into the past simple or the past continuous.**

1 By the time the train ...._left_........ (leave), it ......_was getting_...... (get) dark.

2 I .... (still look) for my seat when the train .... (stop) for the first time.

3 I .... (meet) a family from Scotland, who .... (go) to a wedding in France.

4 In the evening I .... (sit) in the buffet. I .... (not eat) much but I .... (talk) to some interesting people.

5 When I .... (wake up) in the morning, we .... (travel) through the vineyards.

6 As soon as we .... (cross) the border, I .... (begin) to feel excited.

7 When we .... (reach) the mountains, we .... (know) our journey was almost over.

8 The train .... (arrive) late and my friends .... (not wait) for me so I .... (take) a taxi to their flat.

Past perfect and past perfect continuous tenses

❷ **For each gap, choose a verb from the box and put it into the past perfect or the past perfect continuous.**

| feel | forget | own | stand up | try | ~~wait~~ |

1 The crowd _had been waiting_ for over an hour for the match to begin.

2 We .... to open the door for five minutes when Ali found her key.

3 When he died, my grandfather .... the business for more than 50 years.

4 David .... unwell for a few days so he went to the doctor's.

5 Katrina was really angry with me because I .... to tell her the change of plan.

6 I was really pleased to sit down as I .... at work all day.

Past simple, past continuous, past perfect and past perfect continuous

❸ **For each gap, put the verb in brackets into the past simple, past continuous, past perfect or past perfect continuous.**

Last week I (1) ..._went_... (go) to the mountains with my cousins. None of us (2) .... (ever ski) before so we (3) .... (look) forward to it for months. While we (4) .... (drive) to the airport, it (5) .... (start) to snow and we were really excited. But when we (6) .... (get) off the plane in the mountains, there (7) .... (not be) any snow at all. Everyone there (8) .... (say) it was too warm for snow. We (9) .... (go) to bed feeling sad that we wouldn't be able to ski. But when we (10) .... (get) up the next morning and (11) .... (look) out of the window we realised that it (12) .... (snow) all night and we would be able to ski after all.

Used to

❹ Rewrite the sentences below, replacing one of the verbs in the past simple with *used to*.

1 Joelle played the guitar in a band when she was at college.
   Joelle used to play the guitar in a band when she was at college.

2 My father's family owned a cottage by the sea. The last time we went there I was 16.
   ....
   ....

3 In the 1950s, most people travelled by bus and train but this soon changed as car ownership grew.
   ....
   ....

4 That's the house where I lived before we moved to the city.
   ....
   ....

5 Nicholas didn't go to the gym so often when he had to commute.
   ....
   ....

6 The library was much busier before everyone had the internet.
   ....

Vocabulary

Suffixes

❶ Make adjectives from the nouns in brackets.

1 I want to be ....*famous*........ one day. (fame)

2 That snake is .... (poison)

3 Greta is doing .... research. (science)

4 This fish is too .... (salt)

5 Peter is a .... children's author. (success)

6 The children are so .... (energy)

7 The film had a very .... ending. (drama)

8 My new neighbour is very .... (friend)

9 My teacher wasn't .... when I explained why I was late. (sympathy)

10 Ali is very selfish and .... (thought)

Travel words

❷ Complete the crossword puzzle.

(crossword grid)

Across

2 I really enjoyed the watersports and cycling on the .... holiday.

5 You see lots of .... ships in the harbour at Palma before they cross the Mediterranean to Italy.

8 We had a very long .... home as there were a lot of traffic jams.

9 At the beginning of the last century people had to make a long .... across the sea to get from the UK to the USA.

10 If your .... is delayed by more than four hours, the airline will give you a voucher for food and drink.

Down

1 We stopped for a picnic on our .... home.

3 We stayed in the town but went on a different .... every day to places of interest in the region.

4 You can catch a .... to most of the Greek islands from Piraeus.

6 Stay in a .... if you want to save money.

7 Foreign .... shows you different ways of life and gives you the chance to learn new languages.

Reading Part 1

Exam information

Read the text carefully before choosing the correct answer.

You are going to read an article from the internet. For questions 1–8, choose the answer (A, B, C or D) which you think fits best according to the text.

❄ In from the cold ❄

Jim Whyte flew out of Japan after spending four months crossing Siberia.

I got my usual seat on the plane, between the man with a large laptop and the woman with a screaming baby and directly in front of the kicking toddler. On this flight I had the added bonus of being at the front up against the wall which meant no legroom and no view of the movies. I'd read the in-flight magazine for the fifth time and discovered that the films I hadn't seen were being shown on every flight operated by the airline except this one, all before the plane had finished taxiing down the runway.

line 8

The flight home followed almost exactly the route I'd taken since November, flying via Seoul, Beijing and Mongolia to Irkutsk and then across the frozen wastes to Moscow. I looked out of the window for any signs of something familiar but I could see nothing but a sea of frozen trees stretching north to the Arctic Sea. A journey that had taken four months, several visas and huge quantities of thermal underwear to complete now took little more than 12 hours, three lousy films and two airline meals to undo.

As the plane came in to land over London in the late afternoon sunshine, the Japanese and Korean tourists peered out of the windows for their first view through the London clouds of the suburbs round Heathrow Airport with the same enthusiasm I'd had for my first view of Kyoto or Ulan Baataar. After such a long time away, even I found the regimented streets a strange sight.

By the time I'd collected my luggage from the carousel, it was beginning to sink in that I was home. I was no longer some strange exotic creature attracting the stares and attention of the local people and I realised I resented this. At least with my long hair and shaggy beard it was a certainty that I would be stopped at customs. 'What was the purpose of your visit?' I was asked. I was really beginning to enjoy the reaction to my answers, but the customs officer had already had enough of me and let me go. The doors to the arrivals hall sprung open and I was greeted by a sea of smiling, welcoming faces which quickly turned blank again when they realised I wasn't their relative. By the time I'd reached the other side of the hall I'd lost the 'I'm back! Guess where I've been!' look on my face.

Little had changed in the past four months. If you had arrived back from such a journey some years ago, the UK could have been struck by a hurricane and you wouldn't have known about it until the pilot started circling above looking for a place to land. These days email, the internet and 24-hour news mean that, despite your best efforts, it's impossible to completely lose touch with home; well, except when you stay in a tent in Mongolia for a week or so.

It was with a sense of sadness that I unpacked my dirty clothes and put my trusty rucksack in the cupboard. Somehow it just didn't seem right to see a piece of luggage that had spent its whole life travelling through the wilds of the Arctic, Europe and the wide open spaces of Asia, now folded up and confined to a shelf above the towels and bed linen until I set off again.

I loved every minute of the trip especially seeing the northern lights in Abisko, the Trans-Siberian Railway, camping in Mongolia and New Year in China. After a few weeks in Japan I feel I only scratched the surface there. Capsule hotels, electric baths and bullet trains left me speechless. I was left totally exhausted and exhilarated by the experience and can't wait to go back once my bank manager gives me permission. I'm already planning my next journey and reckon that the perfect antidote to crossing Siberia in January is to cross the Sahara in August. What do you think?

1 What does Jim mean by 'I got my usual seat on the plane' in the first paragraph?

   A He preferred to sit at the front of the plane.

   B He always seemed to get the worst place to sit.

   C He had got the seat he had asked for.

   D He liked to sit in the same place on each flight.

2 What does 'this one' refer to in line 8?

   A the airline   **B** the film

   C the flight   **D** the magazine

3 What did Jim have in common with the tourists?

   A He was not pleased at the clouds blocking his view.

   B He was not sure whether he had made a wrong decision.

   C He did not know this part of London very well either.

   D He had experienced the same feelings on arriving in a new place.

4 How did Jim feel after he left the arrivals hall?

   A irritated that nobody was interested in his homecoming

   B disappointed that there was nobody to meet him

   C upset that people weren't friendly towards him

   D annoyed that the customs official hadn't trusted him

5 What does Jim say about keeping in touch while he was away?

   A He would have preferred to be out of contact for longer.

   B He was grateful that he was able to use email and the internet.

   C He would have liked to have received more up-to-date news from home.

   D He was relieved to get emails in some remote places.

6 What is Jim comparing when he says 'it just didn't seem right' in the sixth paragraph?

   A his rucksack and the other luggage

   B his dirty clothes and the linen in the cupboard

   C his travels and his home life

   D his past and future journeys

7 Why does Jim say in the last paragraph that he only 'scratched the surface' in Japan?

   A It was difficult for him to get to know people.

   B There is a lot more he wants to see.

   C He didn't understand some things.

   D He found it very expensive.

8 What is Jim's main purpose in writing the article?

   A to explain why he wanted to make the trip

   B to point out the things that can go wrong on a trip

   C to suggest a route across Asia for other people to follow

   D to describe his reactions to the trip coming to an end

Listening Part 1

Exam information

In the exam, you will hear eight different situations. Read the question carefully as it tells you what to listen for.

(4) **You will hear people talking in three different situations. For questions 1–3, choose the best answer (A, B or C).**

1 You overhear someone talking to a tour guide.
   Why is she talking to him?

   A to make a complaint

   B to make a suggestion

   C to ask for advice

2 You hear a man talking on the radio about a place he visited on holiday.
   What does he recommend?

   A the countryside

   B the entertainment

   C the shops

3 You overhear two people talking about a holiday.
   What went wrong?

   A The hotel was full.

   B The suitcases got lost.

   C The plane was delayed.

Food, glorious food

Grammar

So, such, too, enough, little, few

❶ Complete the sentences. Choose A, B or C.

1 I drink **(A)** *too many* **(B)** *enough* **(C)** *so few* milk.

2 I only eat **(A)** *too few* **(B)** *a little* **(C)** *too much* meat.

3 It was **(A)** *such a* **(B)** *so* **(C)** *such* delicious meal.

4 I've got **(A)** *so much* **(B)** *so many* **(C)** *so little* tomatoes in my garden this year.

5 There aren't **(A)** *too little* **(B)** *so few* **(C)** *enough* eggs to make a cake.

6 The pasta was **(A)** *too much* **(B)** *so* **(C)** *such* hard to eat.

7 There's **(A)** *few* **(B)** *little* **(C)** *such* time to cook in the evenings.

8 The market has **(A)** *such* **(B)** *few* **(C)** *so* fresh food.

9 This coffee is **(A)** *too* **(B)** *enough* **(C)** *so much* hot to drink.

10 I don't eat **(A)** *so much* **(B)** *few* **(C)** *enough* vegetables.

❷ Some of these sentences contain mistakes. Correct the mistakes you find and put a tick (✓) next to the sentences which are correct.

1 This is really tasteless. I don't think the sauce was cooked for long enough. ✓

2 It only takes ~~so few~~ *a little* time to make an omelette.

3 The problem is children generally eat too ~~little~~ *few* vegetables.

4 Most of the food we buy in supermarkets has too much packaging. √

5 It's been such ~~a~~ long time since I've had fresh strawberries.

6 She's much too thin. I'm worried about her.

7 There's so ~~many~~ salt in this that I can't eat it.

8 The restaurant wasn't ~~so~~ *as* good as I had expected.

9 He can cook much ~~more~~ better than I can.

10 There ~~isn't~~ *aren't* enough tomatoes for the salad.

Vocabulary

❶ Which adjectives can be used to describe the different kinds of food? Some food will go in more than one column.

meat	fish	vegetables	bread	cheese	milk	eggs	fruit

burnt	fresh	mild	mouldy	raw	ripe

rotten	sour	stale	strong	tender	tough

❷ **Complete the sentences with one of the adjectives in the table on page 16.**

1 I can't eat this steak. It's far too ....
2 This milk tastes a bit ....
  It's been in the fridge for over a week.
3 The bananas are still quite green. They're not
  .... yet.
4 What's that horrible smell? It smells like
  .... eggs.
5 It's great being able to buy such ....
  fish from the market.
6 You can use .... bread to make
  breadcrumbs.
7 I'm not keen on trying that blue cheese. It looks
  ....
8 Children usually prefer .... cheese
  to .... cheese.
9 .... vegetables contain more
  vitamins than cooked ones.
10 The chef cooked the meat slowly until it was
  ....
11 Oh no! The sausages are ....
  I forgot to take them out of the oven.

Circle the sentences with a negative meaning.

❸ **Find the names of ten fruit in the wordsearch.**

N	B	A	N	A	N	M	R	G	Y
E	M	A	N	P	P	L	U	M	R
C	O	C	M	P	O	M	P	L	A
T	L	L	E	L	O	G	E	I	S
A	P	L	L	E	R	R	A	M	P
R	A	F	O	B	D	A	R	P	B
I	P	I	N	E	A	P	P	L	E
N	S	E	P	A	R	G	A	R	R
E	Y	Y	R	R	E	H	C	O	R
S	T	R	A	W	B	E	R	R	Y

1 ....   6 ....
2 ....   7 ....
3 ....   8 ....
4 ....   9 ....
5 ....   10 ....

Writing

A restaurant review

Read some restaurant reviews written by students. Their teacher has made some comments. Match each comment to a review.

Comments

1 The information isn't given in a   **Review** ....
   logical order.
2 The style is too informal.   **Review** ....
3 The use of descriptive language   **Review** ....
   is repetitive.
4 The grammatical range is very   **Review** ....
   simple.
5 It includes irrelevant information.   **Review** ....

Student reviews

A For dessert we had a really nice cheesecake. It was the nicest cheesecake I had ever tasted. It was even nicer than the cheesecake my grandmother makes and her cheesecake is very, very nice.

B *It was my friend's 18th birthday so we ordered a big cake for her as a surprise. As soon as the waiter appeared with the cake, everyone in the restaurant started singing 'Happy Birthday'. My friend was really embarrassed.*

C We complained about the service but the manager didn't seem bothered. I think that's terrible. I mean, if a customer complains, the manager should do something about it. My dad says he doesn't know how a restaurant like that can survive. The food's rubbish anyway; it's not just the service that's bad.

D I like Dylan's restaurant because the food is delicious. The waiters are really friendly and there is a good atmosphere there. All my friends like this restaurant because the food is good and it isn't expensive.

E *It's an unusual place because everyone sits together at long tables, so you have to talk to people you have never met before. There's no menu, only a list of two or three dishes on a blackboard. This means the food is always really fresh. I like sitting with people I don't know because you meet some interesting people that way.*

Listening Part 2

🔊(5) **You will hear an interview with Ivor Roberts, a chef who owns several restaurants. For questions 1–10, complete the sentences.**

RUNNING A RESTAURANT

Ivor enjoys the [responcibility] **1** of running the restaurants, although he also finds it worrying.

Ivor thinks customers return to the restaurant because they want to experience absolute [perfectiin] **2**

Ivor says creating a good [team] **3** is very important for developing a successful restaurant.

Ivor's cooks have to identify the [ingredients] **4** before they make one of his dishes.

There was a problem with a restaurant a few years ago because people only went there for a [celebration party] **5**

Ivor says paying attention to [detail] **6** is how he maintains a consistent level of service.

Ivor likes the fact that cooking is [seasonal] **7**, which means the menu changes regularly.

In [September] **8** they begin to cook richer food.

Ivor doesn't think it's helpful for staff to see an excellent [review] **9**

More than [500] **10** people phone to book a table at Novello's every day.

Use of English Part 4

For questions 1–8, complete the second sentence so that it has a similar meaning to the first sentence, using the word given. Do not change the word given. You must use between two and five words, including the word given. Here is an example (0).

Example

0 This steak is too tough to eat.

ENOUGH

This steak *isn't tender enough* to eat.

1 I'd prefer to eat at home instead of going out.

RATHER

I'd prefer to eat at home .... out.

2 I didn't order a dessert because I was already full.

EATEN

I .... so I didn't order a dessert.

3 My father recommended trying this restaurant.

TOLD

My father .... this restaurant.

4 Our team lost the match because the other team were stronger.

AS

Our team lost the match because they .... other team.

5 'I'm sorry, Madam, the fish has all gone now.'

LEFT

'I'm sorry, Madam, there is .... now.'

6 'I suggest you have the fish,' the waiter said to me.

ADVISED

The waiter .... the fish.

7 There weren't enough eggs to make pancakes for breakfast.

FEW

There .... eggs to make pancakes for breakfast.

8 They only had a little money to spend at the supermarket.

MUCH

They .... money to spend at the supermarket.

Use of English Part 3

For questions 1–10, read the text below. Use the word given in capitals at the end of some of the lines to form a word that fits in the gap in the same line. There is an example at the beginning (0).

EATING IN BRITAIN

More than 500 chefs, food **(0)** ....*writers*........... and restaurant experts have compiled a list of the world's top restaurants. Judges included the owner of two of the most **(1)** .... restaurants in the United States. Their **(2)** .... was that 14 of the world's best restaurants are British.

The judges said that the wide **(3)** .... of food, the number of Michelin-starred chefs and the quality and **(4)** .... of the produce have helped to make the world **(5)** .... of Britain's restaurants. This is quite a turnaround for a cuisine which was once thought of as fairly **(6)** ....

Immigration has also made a **(7)** .... contribution to the British restaurant scene. There are more **(8)** .... cuisines than in any other country.

The interest in British cuisine has been given **(9)** .... in the US as well. America's **(10)** .... food magazine, *Gourmet*, last month named London as the best place to eat in the world.

WRITE

SUCCESS
CONCLUDE

VARY

FRESH
ENVY

INSPIRE

SIGNIFY
NATION

RECOGNISE
BIG

Unit 5 Studying abroad

Grammar

Conditionals

❶ In each sentence, put the verb in brackets into the correct tense.

1   ....*I would enjoy*.... (enjoy) shopping if I could buy anything I wanted.
2   You wouldn't catch cold all the time if you .... (wear) warmer clothes.
3   We'll never finish getting the room ready unless everyone .... (help).
4   You will lose your friends if you .... (not make) more effort to see them.
5   If we .... (want) to improve our quality of life, we will have to use our cars less.
6   Don't miss any lessons unless you .... (be) ill.
7   If I .... (have) more spare time, I would spend it at the cinema.
8   Please contact me if you .... (need) to ask any questions.
9   If I were free, I .... (come) to the concert with you.
10 If you follow the river, you .... (see) the college on the right.

Indirect questions

❷ Marco has just arrived at a language school in Edinburgh. He asks about weekend activities. Rewrite the questions starting with the words given.

1   Does the school organise any activities at weekends?
    Do you know ....*if the school organises any activities at weekends?*....
2   Are there any coach trips?
    Can you tell me ....
3   How much do they cost?
    Do you know ....
4   Where do they go?
    I'd like to know ....
5   Should I put my name on a list?
    Could you tell me ....

Vocabulary

Words often confused

❶ These sentences contain incorrect words. If you need to, use the words in the box below to help you correct them.

                taught
1   I l̶e̶a̶r̶n̶t̶ lots of children how to swim last summer.

2   Your train doesn't arrive till 7.45 so I'll attend you to arrive here at about eight.

3   I assist the same school as my brother.

4   Every student was given a questionnaire to know what their likes and dislikes were.

5   Membership of the sports club didn't cost much so I decided to take part in it.

6   There is a party on the first night of the course so students can know each other.

7   One hundred guests took part in the wedding.

8   We bought two tickets to attend a new film.

attend (x2)	expect
find out	get to know
join	see teach

Study words

❷ Read this conversation between two students. Find the missing words in the wordsearch. Look in all directions.

Max: I'll be so glad when it's the end of
(1) ....

Alex: Will you? Aren't you enjoying your
(2) .... ?

Max: I am. But there have been so many
(3) .... to do. I don't mind
doing the (4) .... but I
find writing difficult.

Alex: Why don't you talk to your
(5) .... ? Mine is really
helpful.

Max: I have and she has been very kind. We
always have several (6) ....
before we have to start writing. And I have
had quite good (7) .... so I
haven't done too badly.

Alex: It's not long now and we'll have finished.

Max: Yes, after three years' studying we'll have a
(8) .... in psychology. Then
we have to find a job!

A	T	W	Q	U	T	Y	R	E	C	B
H	S	X	T	E	A	R	U	T	S	M
G	O	S	I	E	S	T	G	A	L	I
W	R	N	I	R	O	T	U	T	A	U
G	E	I	M	G	H	K	U	Y	I	K
X	S	R	A	E	N	M	R	T	R	U
I	E	A	B	D	W	M	E	E	O	R
T	A	C	O	U	R	S	E	A	T	M
E	R	F	V	R	B	N	I	N	U	Z
U	C	U	C	K	V	E	E	L	T	I
P	H	Y	L	A	J	M	A	R	K	S

Suffixes

❸ ⓐ Make the verbs below into nouns by adding one of the following suffixes: *-ation, -ence, -ment* or *-ance*. Write them in the correct column.

announce	develop	perform	cancel	depend	exist
disturb	imagine	arrange	differ	insure	prepare

-ation	-ence	-ment	-ance
		announcement	

ⓑ Complete these sentences with appropriate nouns from the table. Use the plural form if necessary.

1 There were lots of train .... today because of the bad weather.

2 Bryony is good at writing stories because she has such a vivid ....

3 It is a good idea to buy travel .... when you go on holiday.

4 People didn't know of the .... of the planet Uranus until Hirschel discovered it in 1871.

5 There were a number of letters of complaint about the .... to people's sleep caused by night flights from the nearby airport.

Reading Part 2

You are going to read an article for American teenagers going overseas to study. Seven sentences have been removed from the article. Choose from the sentences A–H the one which fits each gap (1–7). There is one extra sentence which you do not need to use.

Studying Abroad

Shall I study abroad?

Shall I stay at home?

Have you always dreamed of traveling, meeting lots of different people, and maybe picking up a language or two? No matter what country you live in, you can fly over the world's highest waterfalls in Venezuela, learn world trade in Japan, study in France, or take dancing lessons in Ghana.

How? **1** C Semester, summer, and year-long programs allow you to attend school, take intensive language courses, or perform community service in another country. Read on to learn more about study abroad programs.

Besides the excitement of travel, you will experience new customs, holidays, foods, art, music, and politics firsthand. **2** B This is because your viewpoint will be of an active member of the community, not as a tourist.

Another reason for studying abroad is that you'll become more self-assured. Christina studied in Caracas, Venezuela,

a city of 10 million people and a huge change from her hometown of 35,000! Christina says she learned how to be better at standing up for herself and her beliefs and to express herself in another language. **3** D In addition, living away from home can also help you adjust in the transition to college and adulthood. Matthew says when he returned from studying in Australia he was more mature and had a genuine interest in international affairs that really set him apart from his peers. 'After having gone abroad in high school, I found the transition to college to be straightforward – moving 560 miles from home didn't seem particularly daunting after having lived thousands of miles away.'

Although many academic programs abroad have academic requirements, you do not necessarily have to have the highest grades or marks to be

eligible. **4** F Who you are is as important as your academic record. Study programs abroad look for students who are independent, self-assured, enjoy new experiences and different types of people, and can handle challenges.

If you really hate change and don't like the idea of figuring things out all on your own, then studying abroad may not be for you. It's important to be honest with yourself and really think about what you expect. **5** G Of course, if you want to change those things about yourself and don't mind tackling them head on, then studying abroad may be an ideal way to take the plunge.

Are you convinced that a year abroad is for you, but you're worried that your parents will never go for it? **6** A Point out that studying abroad is a chance of a lifetime and that it offers great academic opportunities.

You might also sell them on the idea that students in study programs abroad gain experiences by being in a new culture, broaden their horizons, and increase their maturity and self-confidence levels.

7 H These language skills, cross-cultural experiences, and global outlooks are becoming essential.

A Use some of the points of view that sold you on the idea to explain why you want to study overseas. ~~4~~ 6

B But perhaps more importantly, the different circumstances mean you will learn a lot not only about cultures and people but also about yourself. 2

C You could join a study program abroad, where high school and college students live with a host family in a foreign country. 1

D What could give you more self-confidence than that? 3

E You will have forgotten any doubts you once had about your decision.

F And most do not have language requirements. 4

G You could end up having a miserable time if you don't! 5

H By studying abroad you will have an educational advantage when entering college or starting a career. 7

Listening Part 1

(6) **You will hear people talking in three different situations. For questions 1–3, choose the best answer (A, B or C).**

1   You overhear a girl talking to her father.
    What subject is she studying?

    A history
    B geography
    C maths

2   You hear two students talking about their friend Amy.
    What do they decide to do?

    A talk to her
    B talk to her tutor
    C talk to her parents

3   You hear someone talking on the radio about studying abroad.
    What does he recommend?

    A spending up to six months
    B living with a family
    C socialising often

Use of English Part 3

For questions 1–10, read the text below. Use the word given in capitals at the end of some of the lines to form a word that fits in the gap in the same line. There is an example at the beginning (0).

Abroad with us!	
The company *Study Abroad* was (0) ....*originally*....... founded in 1991 for students who wished to study French in France. Its success led to the	ORIGIN
(1) ....*establishment*.... of other schools around the world.	ESTABLISH
Learning a language in the country in which it is spoken is, of course, a far more (2) ....*effective*.... and faster process than studying in your own	EFFECT
country. It is also an opportunity to mix with local (3) ....*inhabitants*....	INHABIT
and acquire a greater and deeper (4) ....*knowledge*.... of the people whose	KNOW
language you are studying. This makes the whole experience much more (5) ....*enjoyable*.... .	ENJOY
You may wish to attend an Italian language and (6) ....*cookery*.... course	COOK
in Italy or combine a Portuguese course with a sport. You should look at all the (7) ....*possibilities*.... and make the best choice.	POSSIBLE
In order to choose the right course and (8) ....*location*.... for you, we	LOCATE
suggest you contact us to discuss your particular (9) ....*requirements*....	REQUIRE
From the information you give us, we can make some (10) ....*recommendations*....	RECOMMEND

Unit 6 The planet in danger

Grammar

Future forms

❶ Cross out the INCORRECT future form in each sentence.

1 How do you think climate change *will affect / is going to affect / is affecting* your country in the future?

2 In five years' time, no one *will be driving / is driving / is going to drive* 4x4 cars.

3 Next month *I'm having / I'm going to have / I'll be having* solar panels put on my roof to generate my own electricity.

4 *We're going to avoid / We'll be avoiding / We'll have avoided* flying from now on.

5 By the end of the century, many species *will be / will have become / will be becoming* extinct.

6 This government *is going to prevent / will prevent / will have prevented* any more rainforest from being destroyed.

7 I think next winter most people *are going to turn down / are turning down / will turn down* their central heating to reduce their carbon emissions.

8 If everything goes as planned, this time next year *they'll have started / they are starting / they'll be starting* the new recycling scheme.

9 Next year I think *I'm taking / I'll take / I'm going to take* my holidays in this country rather than abroad.

10 Experts predict that the climate *will be / is going to be / will have been* more extreme in the future.

❷ Complete the sentences with the correct future form of the verb in brackets. Sometimes more than one tense is possible.

1 By 2030 we .... *will be driving* .... (drive) cars fuelled by an electric battery.

2 In 20 years' time, I'm sure we .... (not be) so dependent on coal, gas and oil for our energy.

3 Some people say that by the year 2040 the world's oil supply .... (run out), so we need to find an alternative quickly.

4 Now the good weather is here I .... (not go) to work by car unless it rains. I .... (cycle).

5 I doubt people .... (give up) travelling by plane.

6 On the weather forecast they predicted that this summer .... (be) the wettest on record.

7 The government has promised it .... (improve) transport so people .... (use) their cars less.

8 It .... (be) ten years next March since the farm started growing only organic vegetables.

9 We don't know exactly what the effects of climate change .... (be).

10 Soon it .... (not be) possible to drive your car around any of our cities.

Vocabulary

Effects of climate change

Match the effects of climate change to the labels on the map.

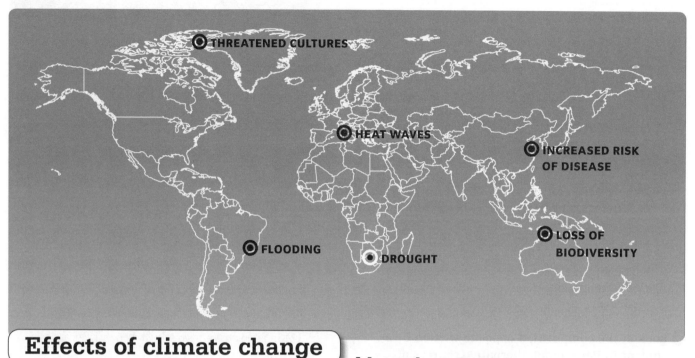

Effects of climate change

1 ....Threatened cultures.................................
Changing snow and ice conditions will force many communities to change their traditional way of life.

2 ....
Rising coastal temperatures could make outbreaks of cholera more widespread.

3 ....
The elderly may be at risk and there could be more frequent forest fires because of longer, hotter summers.

4 ....
A rise in sea levels is projected to cause damage to low-lying coastal regions in Latin America. Fisheries and tourism will also be affected.

5 ....
It is projected that by 2075 between 75 and 250 million people will be experiencing problems with their water supply.

6 ....
Ecologically-rich areas, including The Great Barrier Reef, will be significantly affected with many species at risk.

Listening Part 3

You will hear five different people talking about a new congestion charging scheme to reduce traffic pollution in cities. For questions 1–5, choose from the list (A–F) the opinion each speaker expresses. Use the letters only once. There is one extra letter you do not need to use.

A It will benefit people who live in the city centre.

B It will change people's behaviour.

C It will harm businesses in the city centre.

D It will be unpopular but it's necessary.

E It will have little impact on reducing pollution.

F It will be very expensive to set up.

Speaker 1		1
Speaker 2		2
Speaker 3		3
Speaker 4		4
Speaker 5		5

Writing

Linking words and phrases

❶ Match the two halves of the sentences.

1 As a result of climate change,

A unless more is done to cut carbon emissions.

2 Many people don't take climate change seriously

B this is having little effect on demand.

3 There will be greater numbers of natural disasters

C for this reason it's important to take action now to prevent this.

4 Although the cost of petrol is rising fast,

D many coastal areas are threatened.

5 Many scientists believe climate change may be happening at a faster rate than previously predicted;

E despite the evidence produced by scientists.

❷ Look at the composition opposite written by a student in Peru about alternative sources of energy.

Circle the linking words which could be used instead of the underlined words or phrases (1–6). There is more than one correct answer.

1 (A) In my opinion
  (B) I mean that
  (C) I believe that
  (D) I hope that

2 (A) What's more
  (B) Furthermore
  (C) Moreover
  (D) For this reason

3 (A) because of this
  (B) consequently
  (C) unless
  (D) secondly

4 (A) although
  (B) despite
  (C) though
  (D) even

5 (A) because
  (B) for this reason
  (C) as a result
  (D) even if

6 (A) I feel
  (B) I suggest
  (C) I would argue
  (D) I support

(1) I think that using the wind power to generate electricity is a great idea. Where I live in Lima, Peru, wind power would be a great alternative because of the low environmental impact, but the government doesn't have the resources to make such an investment.

(2) In addition, we have a huge bed of natural gas, and (3) so energy costs are much more affordable.

We can't use solar power in Lima, because the sky is grey (always cloudy), (4) but in other cities in Peru it is sunnier. Many people don't have enough money to pay for electricity in these places; (5) so they buy solar panels (sponsored by the government) and use these to generate electricity. (6) I think that this is a great way to reduce the cost of electricity and to help protect the environment.

❸ Notice how the student uses the adjective 'great' three times in this short essay. Choose a different adjective from the box to replace the 'great' each time.

| fantastic | wonderful | excellent | useful |
| efficient | effective | | |

Use of English Part 2

For questions 1–12, read the text below and think of the word which best fits each gap. Use only one word in each gap. There is an example at the beginning (0).

The effect of climate change on migratory birds

Human-induced climate change has begun to affect our planet and the organisms that live (0) ....on.... it. Many migratory birds are very sensitive to environmental changes and are already (1) .... affected by climate change. Increasing temperatures, changing vegetations and extreme weather conditions lead to significant changes of the birds' essential habitats. (2) .... are the most likely reasons for the dramatic decline in some bird populations and changes in migration patterns.

The ways in (3) .... migratory birds respond to these environmental changes differ across species. Generally speaking, short and middle distance migrating birds can adapt to climate changes more easily, (4) .... long distance migrants (5) .... at a disadvantage. Their migration pattern is usually more fixed and they struggle (6) .... readjusting to changing temperatures. (7) .... of this inflexibility they suffer more (8) .... the impacts of climate change than other birds.

Species that are already in decline are especially vulnerable to climate change. In (9) .... words, climate change may give these already very vulnerable species the final push (10) .... extinction. It is not only in the interest of migratory birds, (11) .... also in our own interest to protect all species (12) .... the impact of climate change.

Use of English Part 4

For questions 1–8, complete the second sentence so that it has a similar meaning to the first sentence, using the word given. Do not change the word given. You must use between two and five words, including the word given. Here is an example (0).

Example:

(0) There won't be any oil left soon.

RUN

We will .....*run out of*..... oil soon.

1 I'm still optimistic about climate change although the predictions are depressing.

DESPITE

I'm still optimistic about climate change .... predictions.

2 Endangered species will become extinct if we don't do more to protect them.

UNLESS

Endangered species will become extinct .... to protect them.

3 Rising sea levels are a real threat to many coastal regions.

RISK

Many coastal regions .... rising sea levels.

4 Governments have done too little to protect the environment.

ENOUGH

Governments .... to protect the environment.

5 I always travel to work by train so that I don't waste time in traffic jams.

AVOID

I always travel to work by train .... traffic jams.

6 It hasn't rained for six months.

SINCE

It .... it rained.

7 The lake always used to freeze over in the winter.

WOULD

The lake .... in the winter.

8 He left before the thunderstorm started.

ALREADY

He .... the thunderstorm started.

Unit 7 My first job

Grammar

Countable and uncountable nouns

❶ **Choose a word from the box to go in the gap in each sentence. You will need to make some of the words plural.**

bag	dish	equipment	experience
food	information	luggage	~~meal~~
suggestion	vacancy		

1 There are few ....*meals*........ which can be prepared in less than ten minutes.

2 If you need any climbing .... , that shop over there is the place to go.

3 I had a great trip to Japan – I especially enjoyed the delicious .... and the scenery.

4 If you take a large number of .... onto the plane, you have to pay extra.

5 Jack sends long emails but they contain little .... about what he's doing.

6 I'm looking for a job but there aren't many .... at the moment.

7 Here are a few .... on how to get a job in the music industry.

8 If you come to dinner, I will make you a traditional .... like beetroot soup.

9 You can walk to the hostel from the station unless you have a great deal of ....

10 You might not get the job because you have little .... in advertising.

Articles

❷ **Put *a*, *the* or – in each gap.**

Working in films

You don't need to be **(1)** ....*a*......... famous actor to get **(2)** .... part on **(3)** .... film set but you need to be willing to start at **(4)** .... bottom. For example, you could spend hours standing in **(5)** .... rain by **(6)** .... gate in **(7)** .... field stopping **(8)** .... people from coming in.

In **(9)** .... Britain and most other countries, you should look for **(10)** .... job as **(11)** .... 'runner'. Runners fetch things and help generally. This is **(12)** .... most junior job and even if you want to be **(13)** .... camera operator, it's **(14)** .... good place to start.

You could do **(15)** .... training course but **(16)** .... best qualification is **(17)** .... experience.

Writing

Applying for a job

a Read the question and two students' answers, A and B, below.

You have seen this advertisement for a job in your local English language newspaper.

We are looking for someone to work in our shop near the beach. You should

• have worked in a shop before • enjoy dealing with people
• be willing to work some weekends.

Write explaining why you would be suitable for the job to: Mr Anna Richardson, Manager

Write your letter of application in 120–180 words.

Check whether the students have answered the question. Put a tick or a cross in the boxes.

	Answer A	Answer B
Does the student mention their experience?		
Does the student say they are good with people?		
Does the student say when they can work?		
Does the student say what they are doing now?		
Does the student say why they are suitable for the job?		
Has the letter got a good beginning?		
Has the letter got a good ending?		

b Which is the best answer? Why?

c Neither of the letters has paragraphs. Mark where they should go.

A

Dear Mrs Richardson, I recently saw the advertisement that appeared in the local newspaper on Saturday. I would like to apply for the job in your Sunshine Sports Shop. Firstly I would like to tell you about my experience. Last summer I worked for two months. I was selling pastries and coffee in a coffee shop. I worked there in two shifts, in the mornings and in the evenings for approximately 8–10 hours a day. My job also included cleaning after the shop closed. It means that I know what hard work is. I enjoyed having contact with other members of staff and also with clients. I really enjoyed working with them, meeting new people. I am sure I would be a good worker. Best wishes, Andrzej Tabecki

B

Dear Mrs Richardson, I'm writing in connection with the job advertisement. I am 22 years old and I am currently studying trade and tourism at university. I'm looking for a summer job. I like being at the beach and swimming and recently got a qualification as an assistant life-guard. Last summer I worked in an ice-cream shop at the beach and got used to approaching customers and handling money. I think that my experience will be useful in another shop like yours. Since I train every day, I'm very energetic and strong but I'm also patient and sociable. I will be available any weekday and some Saturdays. I would be happy to provide you with references. I look forward to hearing from you. Yours sincerely, Kyoko Sakamoto

Vocabulary

Words often confused

Six of the sentences below contain an incorrect word. Correct them and put a tick (✓) next to the sentences which are correct.

1 I saw a really funny programme on TV last night. ✓

2 I'm not working tomorrow so I'll take the ~~possibility~~ *opportunity* to play tennis.

3 Thirty years ago, people didn't have so many occasions to travel.

4 I've got a job in the Tourist Information Centre over the summer.

5 My father's written a novel and there's an opportunity it might be published.

6 The course will be funny as the other students are friendly.

7 I'll lend you my necklace as it's a special occasion.

8 You should find it easy to get a work as a nurse.

9 Is there a possibility that you could work on Saturday instead of Friday?

10 I've been offered a wonderful occasion to play at a music festival.

Listening Part 1

(8) You will hear people talking in three different situations. For questions 1–3, choose the best answer (A, B or C).

1 You overhear two people talking at the end of the day. Where are they?

  A in a shop

  B in an office

  C at home

2 You hear a man talking on the phone about a job he has been offered. How does he feel?

  A confused

  B relieved

  C surprised

3 You hear a woman talking on the radio about her job. What does she say about it?

  A It's tiring.

  B It's interesting.

  C It's exciting.

Reading Part 3

You are going to read an article about being a newspaper reporter. For questions 1–15, choose from the people (A–D). The people may be chosen more than once.

Which person says

they had a particular advantage when applying for one job?	**1**
time for research is often limited?	**2**
their present job is good training for their future career?	**3**
they find it difficult when they are not permitted to finish something?	**4**
it is important to take advantage of subject areas you know a lot about?	**5**
a wide range of general knowledge is important?	**6**
they try to be really well organised at some times to reduce the stress at other times?	**7**
they had a job which no longer exists?	**8**
it is important not to make mistakes?	**9**
they have an income which varies?	**10**
they have not advanced steadily in their career?	**11**
it is important for them to build links with the community?	**12**
they cannot always research a story in the way they would wish?	**13**
they were turned down by lots of newspapers?	**14**
that journalists should not let their own point of view influence what they write?	**15**

Working in the news

Newspaper journalists or reporters source, research and write stories for publication in local, regional and national press. Four young reporters tell us what it's like for them and offer tips for those who are hoping to become journalists.

A Craig

I'm kept busy all the time and my aim is to keep on top of everything on a Monday and Wednesday so there is less pressure on Tuesday and Thursday which are deadline days.

As a reporter, you really have to be ready for anything. A story could come up on a subject you know nothing about and you may have just half an hour to read a report or past stories before you interview someone. I spend most of my time in the office, unfortunately.

My advice for potential journalists is that you need to be able to speak to anyone in all walks of life. A story could come up where the subject is close to your heart but you have to be unbiased and open to other people's opinions, even if you do not agree with them. Every subject is useful – you need to know a little bit about everything.

B Beth

I would say about 60% of my time is spent inside the office. It is always better to visit someone in their house as it makes for a much better story, but due to time constraints unfortunately this is not always possible.

The experience I'm gaining at a local newspaper will set me up for a job on a bigger newspaper. Local newspapers are a great source of news for national newspapers. The general agreement at my newspaper is that the story can be passed on as long as it has appeared in our paper first. The biggest hint I could give to journalism graduates is not to give up when you are turned down for your first few jobs.

To be a journalist you must be outgoing and professional; you will often find yourself in a situation where you have to generate a conversation with a complete stranger who may not want to speak to you! You also have to ensure accuracy in all stories.

C Andrew

I graduated in 1991 with a degree in film and literature. During my final year I sent my CV and a letter to 40–50 regional papers – and every morning I woke up to another rejection! Then I got a job. I think the editor was impressed by my commitment and also by the fact that I come from the area and know about local issues.

I now work from home on a freelance basis, writing features for the Sunday newspapers. You have to be very self-motivated and able to generate ideas for new stories all the time. In a good week I'll sell two or three features to magazines who pay around £400 – £500 per story. Some weeks I'll sell nothing.

Journalism isn't a profession where you progress upwards from one position to the next. I've made several moves already but it's not clear whether they were upwards, downwards or sideways! You need to be prepared to work hard to get work experience, get a qualification and demonstrate your commitment. If you're a specialist in anything (sport, music, computer games), write about it.

D Deborah

I had no career plan at all when I graduated – I found a job as a darkroom technician, one of the last, with a very small family-owned paper where I found myself doing all sorts of jobs. The paper has since been taken over and many of the jobs I did are now managed by computers. While there I decided to train as a journalist. I must be the only person in the universe to 'fall into' journalism!

A crucial part of my job is building contacts locally. I attend a lot of council meetings to try to find out what is going on with the 15,000 employees and attend numerous other meetings.

Why do I do it? It's certainly not for the money, which is very poor. I really enjoy seeing my words change things. The frustrations include leaving a story I'm enjoying working on because the editor wants something else.

Unit 8 High adventure

Grammar

Infinitive and verb + -ing

1 a Tick (✓) the sentences which are grammatically correct. Correct the ones which are wrong.

1 **a** I started to do paragliding when I was at university.

   b I started paragliding when I was a university student.

2 **a** There was no point to windsurf because there wasn't any wind.

   b There wasn't enough wind for continuing windsurfing.

3 **a** I regret not to finish the race.

   b Deciding to give up racing is something I regret.

4 **a** My uncle suggested taking up scuba-diving.

   b My uncle suggested that I should give scuba-diving a go.

5 **a** I stopped to rest after running for five kilometres.

   b I stopped resting after running for five kilometres.

6 **a** It wasn't worth to go on, the climb was too dangerous.

   b Continuing the climb was pointless because it was too risky.

b Which pairs of sentences have a different meaning?

....

....

....

....

Vocabulary

Phrasal verbs with *take*

Look at the phrasal verbs and their definitions. Then complete the sentences with the correct verb.

take sthg up	to start a new hobby or activity
take to sthg	to be good at, or enjoy something new
take after	to be similar to a member of your family
take off	to be a success, become established
take sthg on	to accept new challenges or responsibilities

1 I take .... my father. He was scared of heights too.

2 I've been asked to take .... the role of group leader on the next climbing expeditions.

3 Her career as an underwater photographer has really taken .... Her photos are always in different magazines.

4 I think he should take .... a new challenge. Something like cross-country running would be good.

5 I didn't think I'd enjoy it much but I really took .... snowboarding. It wasn't as difficult as I'd expected.

Writing

Proofreading – spelling

Find the spelling mistakes in this report. There are ten mistakes.

Report on college trip to Brookwood Adventure Centre

Introduction

The aim of this report is to evaluate the recent college trip to Brookwood Adventure Centre and to make recomendations about future college visits to this centre.

College trip, June 19–23

Brookwood is conviniently situated from the college (2 hours by bus) near Bluewater Lake. 20 students from the college spent 5 days there and took part in a sailing course.

The Facilities

The acommodation was very confortable and spacious. The food was excelent, although some students said there wasn't enough choice. There are also cheap restaurants a short bycycle ride away.

The courses

The activities were well-organised and safety standards were high. Students said they enjoyed the course despite the bad wether. Some students thought there weren't enough oportunities to practise sailing but they were all impressed with the instructors, who were all extremely experienced. Each student was given a lot of personal attention wich helped them to develop their confidence.

Conclusion

I belive this course was beneficial for all the participants. It was also good value for money. For these reasons I would suggest organising the same trip next year.

Listening Part 2

9 **You will hear part of a radio interview with Barry Helman, a cave-diving expert. For questions 1–10, complete the sentences.**

CAVE DIVING

Barry says it is the incredible beauty and [1] of the caves that attracts him to diving.

Barry compares himself to an [2]

Other divers say the danger is a [3]

Barry says the most frightening thing about cave diving is the complete [4]

Because it's not possible to get to the surface easily, having good [5] skills is essential for survival.

Most accidents involve people who take [6] when diving.

[7] is a potentially dangerous problem.

You need to have proper [8] to do cave diving.

A good cave diver should never [9] when facing a serious problem.

Barry thinks being a good diver increases your [10] in normal life.

Use of English Part 1

For questions 1–12, read the text below and decide which answer (A, B, C or D) best fits each gap. There is an example at the beginning (0).

Planning an Adventure Trip

Knowing what to expect from your destination will (0) .... all aspects of planning an adventure trip easier, as well as helping you to (1) .... the most out of the experience. Research will help you pick the best places to go but you'll also learn what you need to pack, what health and safety (2) .... to take, and what cultural (and sometimes political) issues you should be (3) .... of.

Climate and seasonal pricing are important (4) .... in your decision about when to go. (5) .... for adventure travel, bad weather or weather you're not (6) .... for can ruin the trip. While you can't predict the (7) .... weather in advance, you can learn about climate (8) .... ahead of time when doing your destination research. Seasonal popularity and pricing should also be considered if you intend to (9) .... peak-season crowds and prices.

While some research is absolutely (10) ...., don't plan every moment of your trip in advance. Over-planning tends to make us less (11) .... to take part in the unpredictable and spontaneous (12) .... that are part of any sort of adventure travel. It's really important to keep a big reserve of excitement and energy ready for the unexpected.

0 (A) make	B do	C ensure	D have
1 A take	B get	C find	D set
2 A insurance	B precautions	C warnings	D information
3 A aware	B familiar	C informed	D knowledgeable
4 A points	B reasons	C factors	D details
5 A Especially	B Exceptionally	C Definitely	D Necessarily
6 A anticipated	B prepared	C expected	D planned
7 A accurate	B correct	C true	D exact
8 A probabilities	B trends	C assessments	D estimations
9 A keep away from	B keep out	C keep off	D keep up
10 A needed	B essential	C ideal	D useful
11 A curious	B interested	C appreciative	D willing
12 A circumstances	B performances	C events	D chances

Use of English Part 2

For questions 1–12, read the text below and think of the word which best fits each gap.
Use only one word in each gap. There is an example at the beginning (0).

What is ski touring?

Ski touring is exactly that – touring on skis. It combines **(0)** ...the... best bits of skiing
and mountaineering and provides the perfect way to explore the mountains in winter.
The advantages **(1)** .... ski touring are that you can really escape the crowds, enjoy
the solitude of the mountains and **(2)** .... rewarded with breathtaking views and
exhilarating descents.

Ski touring involves both going up and going down the mountain; both present challenges,
and new skills **(3)** .... to be acquired. **(4)** .... is much to learn about 'skinning up'
(getting up the mountain) that improves efficiency and saves energy. Similarly you want
to be **(5)** .... to enjoy going down, **(6)** .... means learning to cope with the variety
of snow conditions you will encounter off-piste. **(7)** .... takes a lot of practice. All ski
touring is demanding exercise and you must be **(8)** .... good physical condition. The
fitter you are, the **(9)** .... fun you have.

Rapidly deteriorating conditions and the 'human factor' are the primary reasons
(10) .... accidents. The human factors include stress, complacency, poor
communication, over-confidence and fatigue. You should always ski within the limits of
(11) .... ability, and make sure you know **(12)** .... to navigate properly with map and
compass.

Grammar

Reported speech

❶ Anita asked her friends what they thought about a television programme and wrote down what they told her. Write the words each person actually said.

For my English homework, I want to write about a television programme called 'Life swap'. What do you think about it?

Anita

1 Lucy told me she would definitely watch the whole series.

2 Jessica said her whole family had watched it the day before and they had all liked it.

3 Harry said he had never seen it and he didn't want to.

4 Grace said she was going to watch it the following week.

5 Daniel told me he couldn't wait for the next episode because he was really enjoying it.

6 Charlie said he had only seen one episode and it had been a bit boring but he might watch it again.

1 Lucy: *I'll definitely watch the whole series.*

2 Jessica: ....

3 Harry: ....

4 Grace: ....

5 Daniel: ....

6 Charlie: ....

❷ ⓐ Match what the people said (A–F) to a reporting verb in the box.

admit	announce	complain
promise	~~inform~~	warn

A (The bus leaves at two thirty.)

.... *inform* ....

B (The city centre can be dangerous at night.)

....

C (This food tastes disgusting.)

....

D (I will give the money back tomorrow.)

....

E (I'm going to live in Brazil.)

....

F (I told a lie.)

....

ⓑ Now report what the people in 2a said.

1 The bus driver informed us *that the bus left at two thirty.*

2 Filip complained that ....

....

3 Beatriz promised that ....

4 Paul announced that ....

5 Roberto warned that ....

6 Tereza admitted that ....

....

Vocabulary

Entertainment

❶ Read the clues and complete the crossword.

Across

4 This entrance is for actors only whereas the other entrance is for the general ....

5 The .... was excellent, despite none of the actors being professional.

8 At the beginning of the show, the .... told everyone what the prizes were.

9 That actor was in a historical .... on TV last week.

10 Some famous actors did the voices of the animals in a .... I saw.

11 My favourite actor was only in the first .... of the play unfortunately.

13 I'm a TV .... so I have to make all the practical arrangements for a programme.

14 There were more .... than usual at the football match.

Down

1 I watched an excellent .... about dolphins yesterday.

2 The first .... on last night's quiz show won £10,000.

3 The two singers sang together on .... for the first time for 20 years.

4 The main actor's .... wasn't as good as usual tonight.

6 I love .... programmes because they make me laugh.

7 The .... started clapping as soon as the band were announced.

8 The .... was first performed in this theatre in 1934.

12 I need to watch the .... to find out what's happened in the world today.

Saying what you like

❷ Match the two halves of the sentences.

1 I'm not too keen
2 I don't mind
3 I'd rather
4 I really enjoy
5 I can't stand
6 I'm not interested
7 I prefer

A go to the cinema than the theatre.

B in watching films on TV.

C watching quiz programmes because I like answering the questions.

D to watch films without subtitles.

E watching horror films because I can't sleep afterwards.

F on going to the cinema in the afternoon.

G staying at home on Friday evenings because there are some good programmes on TV.

Reading Part 2

❺ You are going to read an article about a woman who works with celebrities as a fashion stylist. Seven sentences have been removed from the article. Choose from the sentences A-H the one which fits each gap (1-7). There is one extra sentence which you do not need to use.

'I often spend the day shopping'

Actress Helen Mirren

Rachel Fanconi, 35, is a fashion stylist who has worked with stars like David Beckham, Helen Mirren, Sadie Frost, Calista Flockhart and Robbie Williams. She was interviewed by Alex McRae

Fashion styling is basically about making people look nice. I work on editorial photo shoots, styling models for fashion spreads in magazines and newspapers, and I also style celebrities for big awards ceremonies. **1** There's actually a strong commercial element to styling.

A typical day usually starts with me packing up and returning clothes worn at an awards ceremony the night before, then heading out to find new things for my next assignment. Some stylists go through public relations agencies to find clothes. **2** As a stylist, your contacts are extremely important, so I'm very protective of mine. If I'm finding clothes for someone new, I'll call the person first to discuss their likes and dislikes, which helps me to put together a profile. Then I'll spend the day shopping and bring back lots of different outfits for them to choose from.

The best thing about my job is shopping. I hope that doesn't sound too shallow. **3** I work with a big list of people – models, make-up artists, photographers – on various different assignments, and it's lovely checking in with them if I haven't seen them for a few months. You're collaborating together to make something look gorgeous, and when things come together, it's hugely satisfying.

It's easy, however, to get caught up in the glamour of the job. I feel that with any demanding career, it's important to have a balance. **4** My husband and I are both stylists and we try to avoid this. We're great football fans – we go to lots of games and try to keep one part of our lives separate from our jobs.

There are a range of skills you need to be a top fashion stylist. It's not enough to have an artistic eye. **5** For example, if you go to gigs, exhibitions and plays, it will inform your work. During a fashion shoot, you have to be hawk-eyed, ready to swoop on any uneven hemlines. It is important to be really thorough and careful. I take digital photos and print out suggestions of shoe, bag and outfit combinations, to make sure everything goes together.

So the reality is that it's a lot of hard work. If you want to be a fashion stylist, get a qualification under your belt – not necessarily a degree in fashion styling, but maybe in design. **6** Then do work experience with a stylist in the most stressful environment possible – probably fashion shoots for a newspaper – so you learn to work under pressure to a deadline. Try to learn your craft from a stylist you admire, be as professional as you can, and be prepared to do a lot of work for free.

Don't expect to make any money for the first two years. **7** I'm nervous about saying what I earn, because I run my own business, but you get paid per assignment and it really varies. At the top end, stylists working on a television commercial could make £10,000 a day. You could work freelance, or for an agency.

A Otherwise, you could let styling take over your life and become a caricature "fashion" person, in a bubble.

B You should try to find inspiration in unexpected places.

C In fact, you'll almost certainly have to supplement your income with other part-time work.

D I work differently in that I prefer to deal with people directly, and I try to support London designers.

E More important is planning and organization.

F Their clothes are usually loaned, because when an outfit appears in a magazine or on a celebrity, it's advertising.

G That will give you a useful range of skills.

H Apart from that, it's the social aspect of the job which is important to me.

Listening Part 3

🎧 **You will hear five different people talking about a film they have seen. For questions 1–5, choose from the list (A–F) what each person thinks about the film. Use the letters only once. There is one extra letter which you do not need to use.**

A It was boring.

B It was too short.

C It was set in the wrong location.

D The plot was too complicated.

E It was too serious.

F The acting was poor.

Speaker 1	1
Speaker 2	2
Speaker 3	3
Speaker 4	4
Speaker 5	5

Unit 10 Secrets of the mind

Grammar
Modal verbs: certainty and possibility

❶ **Rewrite the sentences in *italics* using a modal verb: *might, may, could, must* or *can't*.**

1 Ryan is behaving very strangely. *I'm sure he's in love.*
   He ......*must be*...... in love.
2 Deborah is looking a bit tired. *Perhaps she's working too hard.*
   She ....
3 He never goes on holiday. *I don't suppose he earns much.*
   He ....
4 She is studying full-time and she has a job in a restaurant. *I imagine that's very hard.*
   That ....
5 That's definitely not her grandfather. *He's far too young.*
   That ....
6 He's just bought a new car and a yacht. *He obviously sold his business for a lot of money.*
   He ....
7 Andy and Sarah aren't speaking to each other. *I don't believe they've had another argument.*
   They ....
   another argument.
8 You seem very familiar. *Perhaps we've met before.*
   We ....
9 She says she doesn't want to have children. *I'm sure she didn't have a happy childhood.*
   She ....
   a happy childhood.
10 I don't know why she didn't tell me she'd left her job. *It's possible she thought I would be angry.*
   She ....

❷ **Read the paragraph about risk-taking. Circle the correct modal in each sentence.**

Psychologists believe that taking risks has always been part of human nature. For early humans, risk-taking **(1) *must / can't*** have been part of every day life. Psychologists think that early human risk takers **(2) *may / can't*** have been more likely to explore new places, possibly finding a new source of water or food. Such individuals **(3) *can't / might*** also have risked doing things differently, such as using a new kind of weapon or animal trap. These acts **(4) *must / mustn't*** have given the risk taker a great sense of achievement, but **(5) *can't / could*** also have profoundly benefited his or her group by improving their lives in some way.

Writing
Beginning and endings

❶ **When you are writing a story it's very important to organise your ideas logically. Opposite is the first paragraph of a student's story, answering the exam question in the box below. It isn't organised coherently. Put the sentences A–F on the next page in the correct order.**

You have decided to enter a short story competition in an English language magazine. The competition rules say the story must **end** with the words:

I had never felt so proud.

Write your story.

Paragraph 1

A There were a lot of boats out on the lake.

B I was taking my dog for a walk as usual by the lake.

C Suddenly I saw one of the boys fall into the lake.

D It started out as just another ordinary day.

E His teacher hadn't seen him and he wasn't wearing a life-jacket.

F I could see a group of young children who were learning to sail.

The order should be: ....

2 ⓐ Now read paragraph 2 and the three alternative endings.

Paragraph 2

Without thinking I jumped in and swam over to him. Fortunately, I had done a life-saving course the year before, so I knew what to do. Someone called for an ambulance and the boy was quickly rushed off to hospital. I had to give my name and address to the ambulance driver.

Ending 1

The next day I received a lot of visitors; first the boy's parents who wanted to thank me for saving their son's life, then a journalist who wanted to take my picture for the newspaper. And finally, a man from the local council who wanted to give me a medal for bravery came to see me. I had never felt so proud.

Ending 2

I was soaking wet and started shaking with cold, or perhaps it was shock. The man from the sailing club gave me a towel and some dry clothes and then I went home. As I was walking home, I started to think about what had happened. It made me feel scared at first because the boy could have drowned but then I started to feel quite proud of myself. In fact, I had never felt so proud.

Ending 3

I phoned my mum to ask her to collect me because I didn't want to walk home in wet clothes. I waited in the sailing club and they gave me a hot drink to warm me up. When she arrived I told her what had happened. Everyone said I was very brave. My mum was very pleased. I had never felt so proud.

ⓑ Which ending:

a) best describes the writer's feelings? ....

b) contains the most complex sentences? ....

c) uses repetition for effect? ....

d) jumps ahead in time? ....

e) gives unnecessary details? ....

f) makes the most impact? ....

Vocabulary

Collocations

❶ Which verbs collocate with the nouns below? Put the nouns in the correct column.

progress	fun	patience	confusion
a shock	peace	chaos	an effort
changes	offence	a mistake	unhappiness

make	have	cause

Adjectives describing personality

❷ Complete the puzzle with adjectives describing personality, by reading the clues below. The number of letters is given in brackets. Which word appears vertically?

1 Someone who puts the needs of other people first. (9)

2 Someone who is considerate of other people's feelings. (10)

3 Someone who is imaginative and has lots of ideas. (8)

4 Someone who is warm and kind. (8)

5 Someone who is relaxed and open-minded. (9)

6 Someone who can be trusted. (11)

7 Someone who enjoys being alone. (8)

8 Someone who enjoys new and challenging experiences. (11)

```
1        U  N  S  E  L  F  I  S  H
2           T  _  _  _  _  _  _  _  _
3              C  _  _  _  _  _  _  _
4        F  _  _  _  _  _  _  _
5           E  _  _  _  -  _  _  _  _
6  R  _  _  _  _  _  _  _  _  _  _
7           S  _  _  _  _  _  _  _
8        A  _  _  _  _  _  _  _  _  _  _
```

Listening Part 4

🔊 **You will hear an interview with a psychologist talking about the science of happiness. For questions 1–7, choose the best answer (A, B or C).**

1 Professor Jackson thinks the scientific studies on happiness
   A are less accurate than economic studies.
   B will be used to measure the success of governments.
   C will become less useful in the future.

2 Evidence suggests that happier people can live for an extra
   A three years.
   B six years.
   C nine years.

3 What seems to be the relationship between standard of living and happiness?
   A People are happier now than in the past.
   B People in rich countries are getting happier.
   C People need to achieve a basic income to be happy.

4 People who buy material goods to make them happy are
   A usually dissatisfied with their purchases.
   B confusing happiness with pleasure.
   C only happy for a short time.

5 What effect do scientists think friendship has on happiness?
   A Having strong friendships may improve health.
   B People with a lot of friends seem to be the happiest.
   C Close friends are more important for happiness than family.

6 What do recent studies say about happiness at work?
   A People need to feel useful.
   B People need to enjoy their work.
   C People need to have goals.

7 Professor Jackson says the easiest way to increase happiness is to
   A smile more often.
   B stop comparing yourself to others.
   C do something kind every day.

Use of English Part 3

For questions 1–10, read the text below. Use the words given in capitals at the end of some of the lines to form a word that fits in the gap in the same line. There is an example at the beginning (0).

Personality Types	
It's often said that no two people are exactly (0) ....*alike,*........	**LIKE**
but according to one (1) .... theory, we all share one of	**PSYCHOLOGY**
sixteen distinct personality types, which are formed by different	
(2) .... of personality traits.	**COMBINE**
(3) .... can be made between personality and left- or	**COMPARE**
right-handedness. Most people are born with a (4)	**PREFER**
for one hand, and all of us are born with a personality type. Experts say	
that we (5) .... develop our personality type through the	**TYPICAL**
course of our lives in (6) .... to our	**RESPOND**
(7) .... and experiences – school or work, for example.	**SURROUND**
However, psychologists (8) .... that personality type	**EMPHASIS**
doesn't explain everything about us and that the	
(9) .... of people with the same personality type is often	**BEHAVE**
(10) .... They also stress that no personality type is	**DIFFER**
better than another.	

Use of English Part 2

For questions 1–12, read the text below and think of the word which best fits each gap. Use only one word in each gap. There is an example at the beginning (0).

The happiest day of the year

A British psychologist says he can prove that the last Friday in June is the happiest day of the year.

Cliff Arnall, a University of Cardiff psychologist specialising **(0)** ....in............... seasonal disorders, **(1)** .... created a formula for finding happiness. The research looks **(2)** .... everything from increased outdoor activity and rising energy levels, **(3)** .... picnics and beach trips with families.

Mr Arnall's happiness formula depends **(4)** .... six factors: outdoor activity, nature, social interaction, positive memories of childhood summers, temperature, and holidays and anticipation of time off.

"At the end of June, the days are at their longest so **(5)** .... are more hours of sunshine to enjoy and it's a time **(6)** .... people have lots of gatherings with friends and family," Mr Arnall said.

"Happiness is associated with many things in life and can **(7)** .... triggered by a variety of events. Whether it's a sunny day **(8)** .... a childhood memory that triggers a feeling of happiness, I think this formula proves that the path to finding happiness is a simple **(9)** ...."

The research **(10)** .... commissioned to coincide with the launch **(11)** .... a photography competition asking people to capture moments of happiness associated **(12)** .... the experience of summer in Britain.

Unit 11 Spend, spend, spend!

Grammar

Expressing ability

❶ Put *can, could* or the correct form of *able to* in the gaps in these sentences. In three of the sentences there are two possible answers so write both.

1 I .....*might be able*..... to give you a lift but I'm not sure yet.
2 I .... (not) swim till last year. Until then I was nervous about going in a boat.
3 I .... see Sarah in the distance. She'll be here soon.
4 I've made the main course for dinner but I've been talking on the phone so I .... (not) make the dessert yet.
5 When I was 14, I .... run from my home to the school in four minutes.

6 .... (you) speak Chinese by the end of the course next month?
7 I .... go to last Saturday's match in the end because my friend had a spare ticket.
8 My brother .... (usually) fix the computer when it goes wrong.

As and *like*

❷ Are *as* and *like* used correctly in these sentences? Correct any mistakes and put a tick (✓) next to the sentences which are correct.

1 As you know, this school has been here for more than 100 years. ✓

2 I bought Jack the same CD ~~like~~ *as* you.

3 Tommy looks as his grandfather did at the same age.

4 As far as I remember, I don't think it was possible to fly direct to Mexico 20 years ago.

5 I really admire Jason as an actor, but I don't really get on with him.

6 A loganberry is a bit like a raspberry but bigger.

7 Your hands are as cold like ice.

8 We didn't talk about the important things as where we would live.

9 The beginning of this film was exactly the same as the one we saw last week.

10 I'm working in Italy at the moment like a tour guide.

Vocabulary

Shopping

❶ Read the definitions and complete the puzzle. They are all places where you can buy things.

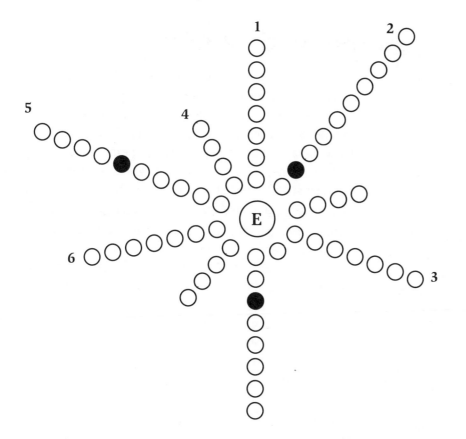

1 A large shop, divided into different parts, each part selling something different.
2 A group of shops, often covered and with its own car park.
3 A shop which specialises in selling clothes.
4 A place selling goods, often food, in an outdoor area.
5 A place where you can buy stamps and send parcels.
6 A small shop selling high quality foods, often from other countries.

Phrasal verbs

❷ Read the text below. Underline the correct words.

LIFE'S LESSONS Andrew, 25

When I moved out of my parents' home into my first flat, I got into big trouble with money. I never looked at my bank statements. I knew my salary was paid **(1)** *back / in* every month but I just took **(2)** *away / out* however much I needed. I sometimes even gave money **(3)** *in / away* to friends who didn't have enough. The stupid thing was that I worked in the foreign exchange department of a large bank so I spent all day checking which currencies had gone **(4)** *on / up* and which had come **(5)** *down / out*. But I never bothered to look at my own account. Of course I soon ran **(6)** *down / out of* money and I started to build **(7)** *on / up* a large debt. I realised that I had to cut **(8)** *back / off* and go **(9)** *out / without* some things. Eventually I paid **(10)** *out / off* my debt. Now I sit down every month and add **(11)** *up / up to* how much I've spent and compare it with how much money I have.

Reading Part 2

You are going to read an article about the psychology of shopping. Seven sentences have been removed from the article. Choose from the sentences A–H the one which fits each gap (1–7). There is one extra sentence which you do not need to use.

Who's playing mind games with you?

Designing a shop is a science, as we found out when we did some research

A bit of retail therapy is supposed to be good for you. You stroll round the shops at leisure, try on items which catch your eye, make those purchases you've been meaning to get for ages. But who's really making the choices? You're certainly picking up the bill, but the shops could be having a bigger say than you think.

We all know how supermarkets use the smell of baking around the store to draw shoppers in and how soothing music can make you stay longer while faster tunes are designed to keep you on the move. **1** Tim Denison, who is a retail psychologist, confirmed this increase and he let me in on some of the secrets of the retail sector.

The shops are clearly far more sophisticated than you might think. **2** In fact this can start before you even get that far, with warm air over the doorway to encourage you in. Of course, that wouldn't work in hot countries. They have their own version with air conditioning at the entrance.

Smells are still a favourite – travel agents sometimes release a coconut odour to get you in the holiday mood. Items placed at eye level are supposed to sell better, and the end-of-aisle displays are best for persuading people to buy food they hadn't intended to. **3** You're then more likely to stop and buy something. Colours are also used successfully: a red carpet is thought to get you in the right mood for spending, while blue is too much like water, and could make you feel uneasy. 'We tend to spend longer on a red carpet than a blue one,' says Tim.

But where the art is really catching on is in the way it differentiates between women and men. A woman entering a shop might well find party clothes, with lots of frills and special materials, at the front. 'The key to effective retailing for women,' explains Tim 'is to make the buying of clothes an engaging experience.' **4** They will be grouped not by what they are but their style – classic or casual, for instance.

When men go shopping it's a different ball game. They want to buy a pair of jeans because their old ones have worn out. In fact, they probably want to get exactly the same jeans. **5** So menswear shops are laid out with everything in its place and men can buy what they want and go – shirts all together here, trousers over there, shoes along there. 'We all know that men hate shopping,' says Tim, 'so what we have to do is make it as simple and spartan as we can.'

6 They say that people want things made easy for them in today's 'cash rich, time poor' society. That's why strawberries and cream are put together – to save people the trip between the fruit and the dairy sections. There's no doubt that some of these techniques work but it's a real science to work out what goes where, with complex financial spreadsheets used to help make the decisions.

But just as the shops are becoming more sophisticated, so are the shoppers. If you're looking for a flat to buy or rent and you notice the smell of freshly brewed coffee, you're likely to get suspicious because this is an old trick to convince people it's a nice place to live. So while the mind games are targeting our subconscious, they tend to work well. **7** We don't mind spending our hard-earned cash, but we want to feel we're making the choices, not them.

A Retailers would argue that they're meeting our needs.

B Such items are placed near each other so they can be visualised together, as an outfit.

C These kinds of techniques have been around for a while, but there's evidence that their use is growing.

D When those decisions are made for us, it can stop us from buying anything at all.

E You spend longer turning corners with awkward trolleys, so they catch your eye.

F These shoppers don't want to be faced with ideas and suggestions.

G But if they become too obvious, we're likely to resist, and things can backfire for shop-owners.

H The minute you walk through their front doors, most of your senses are attacked.

Listening Part 1

🎧 **You will hear people talking in three different situations.**
For questions 1–3, choose the best answer (A, B or C).

1   You hear a woman talking to her son.
   Why is she talking to him?

   A to refuse permission

   B to make a suggestion

   C to give a warning

2   You overhear a teenager talking to a shop assistant.
   What does he want to do?

   A get a refund

   B try something on

   C exchange something

3   You overhear two people talking.
   Where are they?

   A in a post office

   B in a bookshop

   C in a supermarket

Unit 12 Staying healthy

Grammar
Relative clauses

❶ ⓐ Complete the sentences with the correct relative pronoun from the box.

which	who	whose	where

1 There are a lot of after-school sports activities at my school but the people .... most need exercise don't go.

2 Schools .... provide relaxation classes for students get better exam results.

3 At my school .... there are many children from refugee families they need to do more to get girls interested in sport.

4 The diet .... children had thirty or forty years ago was much healthier.

5 The government .... job it is to promote healthy eating is not doing enough to encourage parents to change their shopping and cooking habits.

6 It's the unhealthy options on our school menu .... are always the cheapest.

7 Childhood obesity .... is now a huge problem in Europe may have a significant impact on life expectancy.

8 There aren't many sports activities available for boys .... aren't interested in football.

9 The biggest problem .... many schools have is preventing pupils from bringing unhealthy snacks into school.

10 Having a place .... children can do sports outside school is also really important.

ⓑ Add commas to the sentences containing non-defining relative clauses.

ⓒ Which relative pronouns can be replaced by 'that'?

ⓓ Which relative pronouns can be omitted?

❷ Match the two halves of the sentences.

1 The doctor, whose name I can't remember ...

2 The doctor recommends that I eat less meat ...

3 The treatment I've been having ...

4 I don't know where ...

5 People who are over the age of 50 ...

6 Supplements of vitamin C, which help to fight infection ...

A doesn't seem to be working.

B need to have a check-up every year.

C I caught this cold.

D gave me some good advice.

E should be taken during winter.

F which I will find very difficult.

1 .... 2 .... 3 ....

4 .... 5 .... 6 ....

Writing

Developing your argument

1 Read the first draft of a student's answer to this essay and the teacher's comments.

> You have been doing a project comparing people's eating habits today with the past. Your teacher has asked you to write an essay giving your opinions on the following statement:
>
> *Children's diets are unhealthier today than in the past.*

Give an example.

There is a lot of evidence to show that children's diets are unhealthier today than in the past. **(1)** Today children's diets are unhealthier than in the past because they eat too many unhealthy snacks. **(2)**
In the past children didn't buy so many snacks **(3)**.

Explain why this is a problem.

Explain why not.

Children's diets are also unhealthier because they eat too much fast food **(4)**. Nowadays a lot of mothers don't have time for cooking **(5)** so they buy supermarket meals to put in the microwave instead. In the past people didn't have microwaves.

On the other hand, children's diets have improved a lot in the last 50 years. **(6)**
There is a lot of information for parents about the kinds of food they should give their children. **(7)** Children are also taught about the importance of a good diet in school.

What is wrong with fast food?

Explain why not.

In what way?

Give an example.

2 Now match the sentences/clauses from the student's second draft (A–H) to the correct part (1–7) of the essay. There is one extra sentence which does not match.

A Most tins and packets that we buy today, for example, have labels on them saying exactly what they contain.

B which is bad for their health because this type of food isn't fresh and contains too much sugar, fat and salt.

C This means children don't eat as much healthy food as they should and so many of them are overweight.

D For example, children see these snacks advertised on television.

E Although many children in some countries still suffer from malnutrition, in richer countries most parents can afford to buy meat and fresh fruit for their children, which was not possible for a lot of families in the past.

F A good example of this is the fact that in many parts of the world childhood obesity has increased dramatically recently.

G because they have full-time jobs

H because they didn't have as much money as children today.

1 .... 2 .... 3 .... 4 .... 5 .... 6 .... 7 ....

Vocabulary

Parts of the body

❶ Find the words for these parts of the body in the wordsearch.

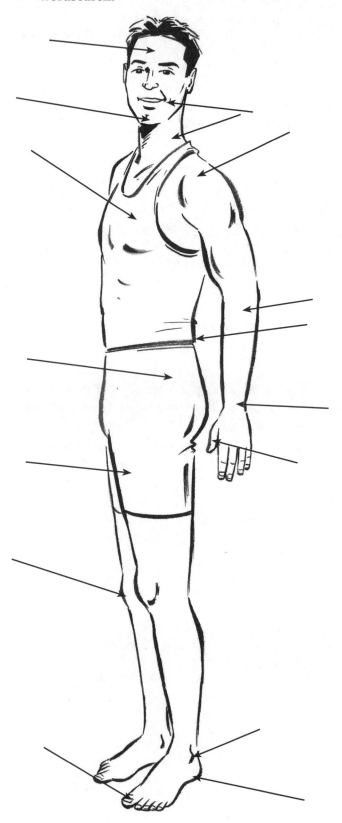

C	H	E	A	N	K	L	E	X	C
E	L	B	O	W	N	O	Y	R	H
Y	E	R	T	E	E	U	E	O	I
T	K	N	C	H	E	S	T	C	N
H	E	E	L	W	R	I	S	H	T
I	B	S	H	O	U	L	D	E	R
G	T	O	I	N	G	O	N	E	L
H	H	O	P	N	T	O	E	K	I
M	U	F	D	E	W	R	I	S	T
C	M	O	P	C	H	E	S	H	P
O	B	A	C	K	I	Y	O	E	I
M	E	F	O	R	E	H	E	A	D

Wordbuilding

❷ ⓐ What are the noun forms of these adjectives?

possible ....*possibility*..........

satisfied ....

respected ....

capable ....

patient ....

obedient ....

able ....

pleased ....

secure ....

ⓑ Now write the negative of the noun forms in the correct column. One word has two negative forms.

dis	im	in
	impossibility	

Listening Part 4

🔊(13) You will hear a high school student interviewing a doctor as part of his research for a project on sleep. For questions 1–7, choose the best answer (A, B or C).

1 People in the past used to sleep on average
   A 7½ hours per night.
   B 8 hours per night.
   C 9 hours per night.

2 A natural pattern of sleep includes
   A one long sleep at night.
   B a nap in the afternoon.
   C frequent short sleeps.

3 Research has already shown that a lack of sleep can affect teenagers'
   A long-term health.
   B performance at school.
   C emotional well-being.

4 What does the doctor say is to blame for teenagers not getting enough sleep?
   A poor diet
   B lack of exercise
   C lack of discipline at home

5 What advice does the doctor give for teenagers who have trouble getting to sleep?
   A read a favourite book
   B listen to music
   C drink hot chocolate

6 What does the doctor recommend schools should do?
   A shorten the school day
   B offer classes in the evenings
   C start lessons later

7 The doctor says that the brain can solve problems
   A if you write them down before sleeping.
   B during sleep.
   C just after waking up.

Use of English Part 4

For questions 1–8, complete the second sentence so that it has a similar meaning to the first sentence, using the word given. Do not change the word given. You must use between two and five words, including the word given. Here is an example (0).

Example:

0 Children's diets are not as healthy as they used to be.
   MORE
   Children's diets are ...*more unhealthy than*... they used to be.

1 The doctor said I should give up smoking.
   ADVISED
   The doctor ....
   smoking.

2 You won't lose weight unless you stop eating junk food.
   IF
   You won't lose weight ....
   eating junk food.

3 Parents who have overweight children, should be given special help.
   WHOSE
   Parents .... should be given special help.

4 'Why don't we go for a jog?' Mike said.
   SUGGESTED
   Mike .... for a jog.

5 I expect people ate more vegetables in the past.
   MUST
   People .... in the past.

6 I didn't start playing tennis until I was fifteen.
   WHEN
   I started .... fifteen.

7 'I'll give you a check-up next week,' said Amy's doctor.
   TOLD
   The doctor .... give her a check-up the following week.

8 Ella was so tired she couldn't study properly.
   TOO
   Ella .... study properly.

Unit 13 Animal kingdom

Grammar

Third conditional

❶ Complete these sentences about the morning when Rose met her husband.

1

I can't walk to work. I'm too late

Rose: If ...I had woken up... (wake up) earlier, I ...would have walked... (walk) to work.

2

The car won't start so I can't drive to work.

Rose: If my car .... (start), I .... (drive) to work.

3

I didn't run fast enough.

Rose: I .... (catch) the bus if I .... (run) faster.

4

There aren't any empty seats so I can't sit down.

Rose: I .... (sit down), if there .... (be) some empty seats.

5

I'm bored.

Rose: If I .... (not feel) bored, I .... (not chat) to the man standing next to me.

6

I'm glad I caught the bus that day.

Rose: If I .... (not catch) that bus, I .... (not met) my husband.

Wish and hope

❷ Put wish or hope into each sentence.

1 I ......hope...... you understand what I'm trying to say.
2 My class has entered a competition and we .... we've won first prize.
3 I .... you could come to New York with us but I know your parents won't let you.
4 I .... Yusuf will be back in time for dinner because I've cooked his favourite meal.
5 I .... I'm not disturbing you but I need to talk to you.
6 We all .... you were here because we miss you.
7 I .... someone would invent a mobile phone that would work everywhere.
8 I .... you had a good time on your trip to Thailand.
9 I .... I hadn't said exactly what I thought.
10 I .... Anton wouldn't watch TV all the time.

Same meaning or different?

❸ If a pair of sentences has the same meaning, put a tick next to them. If they have different meanings, rewrite the second sentence so it means the same as the first.

1 a What a pity I didn't bring my camera.

   b If only I ~~hadn't~~ *had* brought my camera.   ✗

2 a I would like the elephants to come closer.

   b I wish the elephants had come closer. ....

3 a It's a shame we didn't see any giraffes.

   b If only we had seen some giraffes. ....

4 a We made a lot of noise so we didn't see many animals.

   b If we had made a lot of noise, we would have seen more animals. ....

Vocabulary

Name and *call*

Circle the correct word in each sentence. In some sentences, both words are possible.

1 We travelled with a company which is (called) / *named* Africa Adventures.

2 Our guide told us to *call* / *name* him Dego.

3 When my mother was born they *called* / *named* her after her grandmother.

4 What's your brother *called* / *named*? I've forgotten.

5 I saw the advert in a magazine *called* / *named* Explorer.

6 They *called* / *named* their new boat 'Lucky'.

Writing

Giving advice

Look at the beginnings of five sentences below. Choose endings from A–E to give advice about visiting Yellowstone Park in the USA. There are several possible answers. Then put one sentence into each gap in the email.

1 I'd advise you

2 Make sure that you

3 The best idea is

4 You should always

5 If I were you,

A I'd check if any paths are closed before you set out.

B to wear a bell.

C to carry lots of water with you.

D tell someone where you are going.

E walk with other people.

Example: *I'd advise you to wear a bell.*

Dear Irena

You said in your last email that you're going to Yellowstone Park in the USA for a holiday. I went there last year and I know you'll have a good time.

But don't forget that Yellowstone is bear country. While you're walking make a lot of noise which frightens the bears away. (1) .... Some parts of the park are shut in spring and early summer. (2) .... The other thing to remember is that most of the park is wild. It can be dangerous to be on your own. (3) .... Even if you are in a group it's really important that you plan your route. (4) .... It can get very hot. (5) ....

Here's a photo of me in Yellowstone. It's a beautiful place.

Love Meg

Reading Part 1

You are going to read an article from a magazine. For questions 1–8, choose the answer (A, B, C or D) which you think fits best according to the text.

African Safari

Martin Symington went on a camping safari holiday with his wife and three teenagers

We stood silently under the stars, just metres from our tent, hardly daring to breathe. Adam, one of the camp staff, swept a torch beam across a clearing where four impala stood, panicky on their nimble legs. Could they sense the danger they were in? Did they know, as we did, that a female leopard lay under a thorn bush?

She sprang. Four shadowy shapes bounced into the woods. Had the leopard made a successful kill? We all had our theories, but in truth the whole scene had taken place too quickly, and in insufficient light, for any of us to be sure. Now we understood why we had been warned not to go out of our tent after dark, except when accompanied by a staff member. If fact, we had been on our way from the tent to the supper-time camp-fire when Adam's torch had unexpectedly caught the leopard's glinting green eyes. Half an hour later we had a tale to outdo most told around the fire. 'This has got to be the best nightlife in the world,' replied Toby, when some middle-aged fellow safari enthusiast asked him how he was enjoying his holiday.

So much for the assortment of self-appointed experts who doubted that safaris and teenagers would be a workable mix. True, this is a difficult age, with adolescents beginning to sense that they are too old for family holidays. But nor did ours want to return to beach resorts with the kind of 'teen clubs' they wouldn't be seen dead in. So, my wife Hennie and I reckoned, if we were going to have one really good family holiday, why not Africa?

Our holiday began with a flight to Arusha airport, then a long drive to West Kilimanjaro Camp – a semi-permanent gathering of explorer-style tents near the base of the great volcano which was to tease us with rare glimpses of her snowy summit which is 5,895 metres high.

We were introduced to Emmanuel Kinayet, our guide who led us on daily bush walks. Our children wanted to ask Emmanuel a thousand questions about himself and his life, but soon realised that was the wrong approach. Rather, his story seeped out by degrees as he escorted us through his homeland, stopping at places such as a muddy waterhole and a herders' settlement of huts.

Next we took to the hot African sky in a small plane and headed south. Unlike in West Kilimanjaro, there is no human population in the Ruaha other than a lodge for the park rangers, and four small safari camps. We chose to stay at Mdonya Old River Camp, because this is one that avoids luxuries such as soft beds and fluffy towels; these, to my mind, can become obstacles to connecting with nature in the raw. Instead, the five of us shared a simple, yet adequate, tent at the edge of a dried-up sand river.

If there was one disappointment about the wildlife viewing in Tanzania, it was that game drives are not permitted in any of the country's national parks after dusk. But if anything, **this** made our night-time meeting with the leopard and impala outside our tent even more special, bringing home to us the rewards of staying at camps where there are no fences, distractions or even electricity.

By day we mixed game drives with walks through the bush under the protection of our guide Esau for the time we spent in Ruaha. He taught us about bush safety: stay attentive and at a distance from the wildlife, and always stand still if you see an animal approaching you. We spotted only plant-eating animals – elephant, zebra and a pair of giraffes – but we all listened carefully to his repeated message to 'remember that you will see less than one per cent of what sees you'.

Our final hop was over to Zanzibar where we sailed out to a sandbank, swam through bright yellow and pink-and-blue fish and watched a crimson sun set. And we concluded that if there is one family holiday that will have undying teen appeal, it is a safari.

line 5

1 How did the family feel when they were sitting round the camp-fire?

A interested in the stories of the other campers

B proud of what they had seen earlier

C sorry they had disturbed the leopard

D annoyed they didn't know what happened in the end

2 Why did the writer and his wife decide to choose a safari holiday in Africa?

A They didn't want to be with other families.

B They wanted their children to learn some independence.

C They wanted to do something different from usual.

D They were advised that teenagers often enjoy safaris.

3 What does the writer say about Mount Kilimanjaro?

A They were hardly ever able to see the top of it.

B They would have preferred to camp higher up it.

C They were surprised at how cold it must be at the top.

D They realised how difficult it would be to climb to the top.

4 What does the writer mean by 'his story seeped out by degrees'?

A He answered their questions but said no more.

B He didn't tell them everything about himself all at once.

C He told them only the most interesting parts of his life story.

D He had a story to tell about every place they stopped.

5 They chose the Mdonya Old River Camp because

A there was water nearby.

B it wasn't easy to get to.

C the tents were of good quality.

D it was fairly basic.

6 'this' in line 51 refers to

A the dusk

B a rule

C their disappointment

D a plan

7 What did Esau warn them about?

A There were many more animals than they could actually see.

B They should move slowly if an animal came towards them.

C They shouldn't go into the bush alone on foot.

D Some animals were more dangerous than others.

8 Which of the following describes how the writer felt about the holiday?

A unsure whether they would come back again

B frustrated they hadn't seen more animals

C relieved they hadn't been attacked

D satisfied the children had enjoyed it

Listening Part 2

(14) **You will hear a woman called Kirsty Willis, who works in a zoo, talking about careers with animals on the radio. For questions 1–10, complete the sentences.**

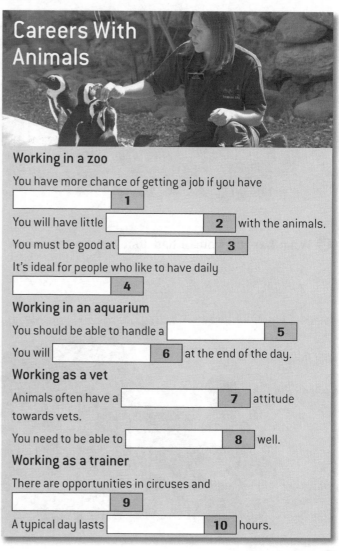

Careers With Animals

Working in a zoo

You have more chance of getting a job if you have ⬚ 1

You will have little ⬚ 2 with the animals.

You must be good at ⬚ 3

It's ideal for people who like to have daily ⬚ 4

Working in an aquarium

You should be able to handle a ⬚ 5

You will ⬚ 6 at the end of the day.

Working as a vet

Animals often have a ⬚ 7 attitude towards vets.

You need to be able to ⬚ 8 well.

Working as a trainer

There are opportunities in circuses and ⬚ 9

A typical day lasts ⬚ 10 hours.

Unit 14 House space

Grammar

Causative *have*

1 ⓐ What does the woman need to have done?
Complete the sentences with the verbs in the box.

clean	remove	replace	fix	cut

1 She needs ...... *to have* ...... the roof
...... *fixed* ....

2 She wants .... the windows
....

3 She is going .... the hedge
....

4 She would like .... the rubbish
....

5 She thinks she should .... the gate
....

ⓑ What has the woman had done? Write sentences.

6 ...*She has had the roof fixed*... .

7 ....

8 ....

9 ....

10 ....

Expressing obligation and permission

❷ Circle the correct words in each sentence.

1 (*You're not supposed to*)/ *You are allowed to* bring your dog into this building but it won't matter if no one sees him.

2 *I needn't have bought / I didn't need to buy* a washing machine for my new apartment. I'll have to sell it on e-bay.

3 My parents *weren't allowed to have / wouldn't let me have* a TV in my bedroom, which meant I used to read a lot.

4 You *don't have to / mustn't* carry that heavy box up the stairs. There's a lift over there.

5 We *can't / needn't* play loud music after 11 pm, or the neighbours will complain.

6 You *shouldn't have / couldn't have* left the door unlocked. Go back and lock it!

7 The builders *were supposed to / had to* finish work on the 21st of June but the kitchen isn't ready yet.

8 *Don't let the children / The children don't have to* climb that tree. It's not safe.

9 You *should / must* turn the gas fire off before you go to bed or there could be a fire.

10 My mum says we *should / are allowed to* have the party at our house if we promise to clear up afterwards.

Vocabulary

Collocations: describing where you live

Cross out the option in *italics* which is NOT correct.

1 The new development is *conveniently / comfortably / ideally* located.

2 The neighbourhood used to be quite run-down but in the last few years it has become much more *desirable / fashionable / likeable*.

3 The streets are lined with *trees / traffic / cafés*.

4 The master bedroom on the second floor *overlooks / looks onto / gives an overview of* the garden.

5 Her apartment is quite small but there's *enough / sufficient / convenient* space for one person.

6 The house is furnished very *luxuriously / expensively / richly*.

7 When we first moved in we could only afford *poor / cheap / second-hand* furniture.

8 The design of the bathroom is very *simple / stylish / well-equipped*.

Listening Part 4

🔊 **You will hear a journalist talking on the radio about adults in their 20s and 30s who still live with their parents. For questions 1–7, choose the best answer (A, B or C).**

1 The survey shows that the European country with the lowest number of 'kidults' living with their parents is

  A France.

  B Sweden.

  C the UK.

2 In Southern Europe young adults continue to live at home because of

  A low salaries.

  B close family ties.

  C a shortage of affordable housing.

3 In the USA people are leaving home later because

  A they are getting married later.

  B they have to pay off student debts.

  C their relationships with their parents are good.

4 'Kidults' living at home say the main advantage is

  A being able to save money.

  B having someone to do their washing and ironing.

  C being free from responsibilities.

5 One disadvantage mentioned by 'kidults' in the survey is

  A the lack of time spent alone.

  B worrying what people think of them.

  C being treated like a child.

6 Having adult children at home can be a problem for parents because it can

  A restrict their freedom.

  B be expensive.

  C damage their marriage.

7 The most common source of conflict between parents and 'kidults' is

  A household chores.

  B mealtimes.

  C financial arrangements.

Writing

Adding detail

❶ Read some sentences from an essay a student wrote about her grandparents, kitchen. Then match them to the type of detail they provide (A–F).

1 I always associate the kitchen with my grandmother.

2 The house was built in 1910 and the kitchen was extended in the 1970s.

3 My grandfather prefers to eat in the dining room because the chairs are more comfortable but my grandmother thinks it's too formal in there.

4 There are usually some flowers from the garden on the table and the smell of something wonderful cooking in the ancient oven.

5 It's difficult to choose my favourite dish but most people agree that my grandmother's fruit cake is delicious.

6 She's a very generous person; she makes jam for all her neighbours and gives them cherries and strawberries from her garden.

Type of detail

A providing a description

B making a comparison

C giving an opinion

D giving an example

E providing facts

F describing feelings

1 .... 2 .... 3 .... 4 .... 5 .... 6 ....

❷ Now look at this examination task. Which of the sentences in Exercise 1 do you think would be relevant for this article? Tick them.

My favourite room

Tell us about your favourite room and why it's special for you.

The best article will be published in next month's magazine.

❸ Plan your answer for this task. What type of detail would you include?

My favourite room

Facts?

Description?

Feelings?

Opinions?

Use of English Part 1

For questions 1–12, read the text below and decide which answer (A, B, C or D) best fits each gap. There is an example at the beginning (0).

A writer's room

It may not look (0) .... an office, but that's the point. The (1) .... of having to work all day in an office would (2) .... I never went there. So there are no filing cabinets or piles of mail and no distracting shelves of books. That all gets (3) .... in a couple of cupboards.

All over the flat there are photographs I've taken of (4) .... countries I've visited; in here they're (5) .... of New Zealand – and I keep my travelling hat and my travelling bag hanging here to make me (6) .... that I could pack up and leave at any (7) .... I can't, but it's nice to (8) ....

If I'm doing serious writing I (9) .... to be in here at night with the low energy bulb and the music, typing on a laptop because I don't have a desk and have no (10) .... for one. When I injured my back I used to try writing propped up on a sofa with lots of cushions and pillows, but that never really worked, so I finally saved up and bought the monster black leather chair. I try not to (11) .... anyone else sit in it, because they usually (12) .... to get out again – it's just too comfortable.

0	**A** like	**B** as	**C** such	**D** than
1	**A** knowledge	**B** idea	**C** understanding	**D** suggestion
2	**A** result	**B** cause	**C** mean	**D** show
3	**A** hidden	**B** covered	**C** wrapped	**D** packed
4	**A** various	**B** broad	**C** general	**D** widespread
5	**A** completely	**B** especially	**C** extensively	**D** primarily
6	**A** consider	**B** dream	**C** think	**D** guess
7	**A** moment	**B** place	**C** date	**D** occasion
8	**A** invent	**B** suppose	**C** pretend	**D** believe
9	**A** enjoy	**B** prefer	**C** appreciate	**D** request
10	**A** hope	**B** obligation	**C** demand	**D** desire
11	**A** let	**B** allow	**C** permit	**D** authorise
12	**A** disagree	**B** refuse	**C** reject	**D** deny

Unit 15 Fiesta!

Grammar

Passives

❶ Complete the newspaper article below by putting the verbs in brackets into the correct form of the passive.

Join us at the Festival of Dance

A dance festival **(1)** ...has been held... (hold) in our town every summer since 2000. It **(2)** .... (organise) every year by three local schools and each child **(3)** .... (give) the opportunity to take part in a performance, competition or street parade.

This year's festival will take place on 15 July and will be bigger than ever because £3,000 **(4)** .... (raise) for the prizes and there's more to come, we hope. Last year, 15 prizes of £100 **(5)** .... (award) but this year there will be at least 30 prizes. At last summer's festival, a local boy, Marcus Aston, **(6)** .... (choose) to go into a national competition. It **(7)** .... (hope) that other children **(8)** .... (offer) that chance this year.

At the end of the day, there will be a special performance by the City Schools Dance Troupe which **(9)** .... (form) in 2002 and has won many prizes. They can also **(10)** .... (see) later in the summer at the Victoria Hall and the Thames Festival.

Plans **(11)** .... (already make) for next year's festival so if you would like to help, please get in touch via the website (www.dancewithus.co.uk). If you would like your name **(12)** .... (add) to the mailing list, you can also do that on the website.

The passive with reporting verbs

❷ Rewrite the newspaper headlines as sentences, using the verb in brackets. You will need to add some extra words.

1 **PRIME MINISTER TO RESIGN TOMORROW**
The Prime Minister is expected to resign tomorrow. ....(expect)

2 **New Airport Runway Will Probably Be Built Next Year**
It ....
.... (think)

3 **NEW TEAM HAS BEEN SELECTED**
It ....
.... (report)

4 **FEDERER IS THE BEST TENNIS PLAYER EVER**
Federer ....
.... (consider)

5 **Report Proves this Summer is Hottest for 50 Years**
This summer ....
.... (report)

6 *BONES FOUND ON BEACH BELONGED TO DINOSAUR*
It ....
.... (believe)

Writing

Answering the question

❶ Read the email below and the sentences A–H from different student answers. Which points do they answer? Put them in the correct column in the table.

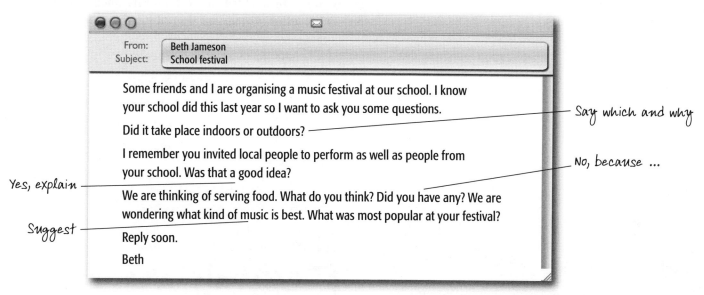

From: Beth Jameson
Subject: School festival

Some friends and I are organising a music festival at our school. I know your school did this last year so I want to ask you some questions.

Did it take place indoors or outdoors? — *Say which and why*

I remember you invited local people to perform as well as people from your school. Was that a good idea? — *No, because ...*

Yes, explain — We are thinking of serving food. What do you think? Did you have any? We are wondering what kind of music is best. What was most popular at your festival?

Suggest — Reply soon.

Beth

A Our school is quite small and we wanted to make sure we had a big audience. The performers brought all their friends with them so that was good.

B You need to have music people can dance to and some music that the students' parents will recognise too, so a mixture is best.

C It's difficult to know how much food to have or what people will eat so it's not a good idea to provide it.

D If the weather is bad, people won't come if it's in the park or on the school field so it's better to be inside. It rained all day when we had our festival.

E The most successful performances were the bands which had young people in them. You could have a bit of classical music too though as some people enjoy that.

F You will probably need to sell drinks but it's very hard work to make food for everyone. You would need lots of people to help so I don't think it's a good idea to provide it.

G In summer, it's nice to be in the fresh air and also you will have more space for dancing so we preferred to be outside.

H We decided we wanted a wide variety of music so we invited people of different ages to perform. You could ask the relatives of the students at your school.

❷ Now write a letter using four of the sentences on the left or your own if you prefer. Here is a beginning and ending to use.

Dear Beth

I am glad to give you some advice about your music festival.

....

....

....

....

....

I hope your festival is successful and that you will tell me all about it.

Best wishes

Say which and why	Yes, explain	No, because ...	Suggest
	A		

Vocabulary

Suffixes

Add suffixes to these words to make personal nouns. Then underline the word which is the odd one out in each case.

1 electric ....   politics ....

    photograph ....   music ....

2 account ....   biology ....

    science ....   guitar ....

3 fish ....   cycle ....

    post ....   police ....

4 report ....   design ....

    manage ....   visit ....

Reading Part 3

You are going to read some texts about different festivals. For questions 1–15, choose from the texts (A–E). The texts may be chosen more than once. When more than one answer is required, these may be given in any order.

Which text mentions

a change due to health considerations?	**1**
specific rules for some events?	**2**
the fact that there is no other similar festival?	**3**
a range of themes within a festival?	**4**
a festival in a place which does not get many international visitors?	**5** **6**
a regional variation?	**7**
an event which had to be cancelled?	**8**
a festival which has recently been lengthened?	**9**
a festival which attracts the attention of the media?	**10**
a festival which is one of the largest celebrations in the world?	**11**
a festival's aim to attract people who would not normally attend such an event?	**12**
an activity which the writer was not good at?	**13**
less interest in a particular tradition?	**14**
how a festival began?	**15**

Listening Part 3

🔊 You will hear five different people talking about something they are going to celebrate. For questions 1–5, choose from the list (A–F) what each person is going to celebrate. Use the letters only once. There is one extra letter which you do not need to use.

A exam results

B promotion at work

C an engagement

D a new job

E a new flat

F a new baby

Speaker 1	**1**
Speaker 2	**2**
Speaker 3	**3**
Speaker 4	**4**
Speaker 5	**5**

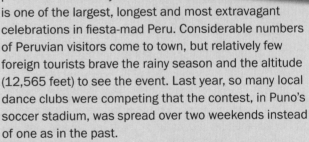

Festivals around the world

A Festival of Candelaria

The festival which takes place in Puno each year is one of the largest, longest and most extravagant celebrations in fiesta-mad Peru. Considerable numbers of Peruvian visitors come to town, but relatively few foreign tourists brave the rainy season and the altitude (12,565 feet) to see the event. Last year, so many local dance clubs were competing that the contest, in Puno's soccer stadium, was spread over two weekends instead of one as in the past.

There is nothing casual about these competitions. Groups must have precise numbers of participants, depending on the dance, and perform for exactly eight minutes in front of a packed stadium of transfixed spectators. After competing, many groups just keep on dancing in the narrow streets of the town.

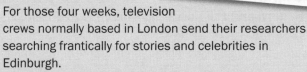

B The Edinburgh Festival

Late summer is the only period in the calendar when the cultural focus of Great Britain really shifts away from London to Scotland. For those four weeks, television crews normally based in London send their researchers searching frantically for stories and celebrities in Edinburgh.

What draws the attention of the international arts world is the extraordinary cultural mix that is the Edinburgh Festival. The scale and range of its ingredients make it unique. Hundreds of events are free, many take place in the street and the festival has always recognised the vital need to involve people with no money and little experience of the arts.

C Chinese New Year

I joined in the New Year celebrations in Pingyao, a beautiful and ancient walled city in central China. Western tourists are uncommon in Pingyao which receives about 1,000 Chinese tourists every week. Dumplings were being made in a local hotel and I was invited to join in and demonstrate my skills over a hot oven. About 30 people surrounded me, cheering and photographing each misshaped dumpling I produced, and I began to feel like a contestant on a TV programme.

Going against tradition, the lantern ceremony was this time on the first day rather than the last of the two-week celebration. A tunnel of fairy lights brought everyone into a large courtyard and the noise of the fireworks was incredible. Lion and dragon dancing was promised, but thelights failed and it didn't take place; the crowd, now very cold, headed for the exit.

D Notting Hill Carnival

West London comes alive to the sights, sounds and colour of the Caribbean on the last weekend in August. For weeks the community centres and homes hum with the sound of sewing machines as the final sequins and feathers are sewn on to elaborate costumes. Soon that quiet sound will be replaced by the beat of calypso and reggae music as the Notting Hill Carnival gets under way.

The event has come a long way since 1964 when the local Afro-Caribbean community took a small steel band procession onto the streets. In recent years more than two million people have taken to the streets of west London, making it second only to the Rio Carnival in size. The costumed parades form the backbone of Carnival, hoping to impress the judges with their interpretation of a chosen topic: aliens, the Wild West and a celebration of black hair are just a few of the storylines to look out for this year.

E The Moon Festival

'We've been working every day now for the last 60 days,' said Johnny Chan. 'We've made about three million mooncakes so far.' Mooncakes mean the Mid-Autumn Festival, or Moon Festival, which lasts for three days.

The Kee Wah bakery in Hong Kong makes dozens of different types of mooncakes. 'The Cantonese-style cakes have a shiny finish, and are filled with a lotus seed paste,' said Johnny Chan. 'In the northern regions, the cakes are less sweet and are often filled with nuts or even meat,' he added. But despite their central role in the Mid-Autumn festival, Mr Chan said that mooncake orders had declined over recent years. Part of the reason, he said, was that people think mooncakes are bad for them and prefer low-fat, low-sugar ones, but also the Moon Festival was becoming more commercialised and people focused more on the exchange of gifts.

Unit 16 Machine age

Grammar

Linking words: *when, if, in case, whether, even if, even though*

❶ Circle the correct word or phrase.

1 *(Even though)/ In case / Whether* my mobile phone was only a few months old, the company wanted to give me a new one.

2 You should always back up your work *if / whether / in case* the computer crashes.

3 *If / When / Even if* I had the choice, I'd buy a huge plasma screen TV.

4 *Even though / Even if / If* you had their phone number, it's still too late to call them.

5 I'm not sure *when / even if / whether* it's worth investing in a new laptop, or not.

6 The company recommends taking out insurance when you buy your MP3 player *even if / if / in case* it gets damaged.

7 They said that *when / even if / in case* the spare parts come in, they'll call you straightaway.

8 *If / When / Whether* you are worried about your children's safety on the internet, then this software will be of interest to you.

9 I'm such a technophobe! I never understand instruction manuals for machines *if / when / even if* they are very simple.

10 *Even though / Even if / When* I explained how to set the timer several times, she still can't do it by herself.

Reporting verbs

❷ Which verbs can be used in the following sentences? You need to think about the verb pattern and the meaning. There may be more than one correct answer.

advise	~~apologise~~	warn	remind	suggest
invite	promise	offer	admit	deny	accuse
recommend	tell	ask	agree	explain	

1 He ..... *apologised* ..... for not telephoning sooner.

2 She .... him to switch off the computer before he left the office.

3 The sales assistant .... I upgrade my PC software.

4 The company was .... of charging customers too much for calls to land lines.

5 The manager .... to exchange my faulty digital camera for the latest model.

6 My brother .... taking my iPod without asking.

7 We were .... not to use our mobile phones in the library.

8 Parents were .... to see the new ICT suite at the school.

9 She .... that she hadn't installed the firewall correctly.

10 He .... her that mobile phones can be a health risk for children.

Writing

❶ Read this student's article for the competition and evaluate it using the checklist below.

A great invention

- **Which invention couldn't you live without?**
- **Why is it so important?**
- **What would the world be like without this invention?**

We will publish the most interesting articles in next month's edition.

A great invention

There have been a lot of great inventions which have affected all our lives. Some of them, such as a map, a ship and a gun have completely changed history. However, I'd say the computer is the most amazing invention; even more important than a car or a telephone.

Nowadays we can't manage without computers, not only at work but also at home. I can't even imagine our world without this 'clever machine'.

Computer plays essential role in office work because it can store huge amount of information. It can help you with your studies, correcting your grammar and training your language skills, for example.

But that's not all computers can do. I have found a lot of new friends thanks to the internet. You can also 'travel' around the world using internet to find out what is happening in a different countries.

I believe that other uses for computers will be discovered in the future. Computers have changed people's lifestyles forever. And they will affect everyone's life directly or indirectly.

---

❷ There are some problems with the use of *a*, *an* and *the* in the article. Decide where these corrections should go. You need to use some of them more than once.

(a) Delete 'a'.
(b) Insert 'the'.
(c) Insert 'a' or use the plural form.
(d) Replace 'a' with 'the' or use the plural form.
(e) Insert 'an'.

This article	YES	NO
1 is easy to read.	☐	☐
2 is divided into clear paragraphs.	☐	☐
3 has a good introduction.	☐	☐
4 has a good conclusion.	☐	☐
5 covers all the necessary points.	☐	☐
6 includes unnecessary or irrelevant information.	☐	☐
7 supports the argument with examples.	☐	☐
8 is too informal.	☐	☐
9 contains both long and short sentences.	☐	☐
10 contains a variety of structures.	☐	☐

Vocabulary

Words connected with computers

Complete the crossword.

Across

1 This may destroy files on your computer.
6 This displays information on a screen.
9 This gives faster access to the internet.
10 This is what you do to files or emails you no longer need.

Down

2 Your computer may not be able to use certain software because it is this.
3 This is when you are connected to the internet.
4 You can put music on your iPod by doing this.
5 If your computer does this you may lose unsaved data.
7 This is where information can be stored.
8 This connects your PC to the printer and the modem.

Listening Part 2

🎧 **You will hear a communications expert talking on the radio about the future of mobile phones. For questions 1–10, complete the sentences.**

MOBILE PHONES

Dr West says that by ⬚⬚⬚⬚⬚ **1** mobile phones will have many more uses.

Mobile phones will be able to warn you about ⬚⬚⬚⬚⬚ **2**

Your phone will be used to make ⬚⬚⬚⬚⬚ **3** for things.

It will also look for ⬚⬚⬚⬚⬚ **4** it knows you will enjoy.

Your phone will know how to deal with phone messages because it knows your ⬚⬚⬚⬚⬚ **5**

It will predict what food items are available in your ⬚⬚⬚⬚⬚ **6**

Using your phone, you will be able to locate members of your family on a ⬚⬚⬚⬚⬚ **7**

Dr West says that your mobile phone will become as essential as your ⬚⬚⬚⬚⬚ **8**

Dr West says more intelligent mobiles need a larger ⬚⬚⬚⬚⬚ **9**

They will also develop the ability to ⬚⬚⬚⬚⬚ **10**

Use of English Part 3

For questions 1–10, read the text below. Use the word given in capitals at the end of some of the lines to form a word that fits in the gap in the same line. There is an example at the beginning (0).

Today, technology aids us in doing even the (0) ...*simplest*...... of domestic	**SIMPLE**
chores but until the middle of the twentieth century most women's lives were	
dominated by backbreaking tasks requiring not only a (1)	**CONSIDER**
amount of time but also a lot of (2) .... Before the	**STRONG**
(3) .... of the electric washing machine, women spent a full	**INVENT**
day or more every week doing the (4) .... laundry. That is	**WEEK**
something which many women today would find (5) .... to	**POSSIBLE**
imagine.	
The electric washing machine was of course a great (6)	**TECHNOLOGY**
success. It was in fact a (7) .... triumph which made a	**DRAMA**
huge difference to women's lives. It represents one of the twentieth century's	
greatest (8) .... advances though it rarely receives recognition	**SCIENCE**
for this. No one who had the (9) .... would ever give up their	**CHOOSE**
washing machine and do laundry the (10) .... way.	**FASHION**

Answer key

Unit 1

Grammar

1 **2** haven't written   **3** 've/have been working
4 'm/am staying   **5** live   **6** think   **7** has/have
always lived   **8** knows   **9** get up   **10** starts   **11** give
12 've/have gone   **13** 'm/am looking   **14** 've/have
been playing   **15** 've/have been writing   **16** 've/have
sent   **17** 's/is always complaining   **18** remember
19 've/have changed   **20** want

2 **2**   Do the children speak English?
3   Do you like the food?
4   Do Diego and Elena often go away?
5   What does/do the family usually do on Sundays?
6   Where does Elena work?

Vocabulary

1 **make:** a decision, a meal, a mess, a noise, a phone
call, a photocopy, a promise
do: your best, a course, homework, a full-time job,
the shopping, a sport, the washing-up

2 **2** made a mess   **3** make a noise   **4** do a course
5 make an appointment   **6** do the shopping
7 made a photocopy   **8** did the washing-up
9 make a decision   **10** make a meal

3 **2** make out   **3** made up   **4** made up

Writing

I definately [definitely] think that teenage year's [years]
should be the best in everyones [everyone's] life because
you can have fun and you have fewer problems than
adults [add full stop]. teenagers [capital T] know how to
have a good time. Most teenagers have a lot of freinds
[friends] and they discuss things that they are interested
in. Teenagers have to be in fashion, [add comma]
wearing up-to-date cloths [clothes] and listening to
modern music. They also like to do sports and compete
in matchs [matches]. But teenager's [teenagers'] parents
sometimes have a difficult time and they dont [don't]
understand why? . [full stop, not question mark]
Wouldnt [Wouldn't] you feel angry if someone went into
your room without permission. ? [question mark, not full
stop] So do teenagers. As teenagers grow up they stop

thinking like children and their believes [beliefs] and
their interests change. My opinion is that teenage years
are magical and Id [I'd] like to stay a teenager forever.

Listening Part 3

1B   **2F**   **3C**   **4E**   **5A**

Recording script   CD1 Track 2

Announcer: Speaker 1

Teenage girl: Every year my family get together and
go down to the river for a picnic. There's
usually about twelve of us – kids and
grown-ups. We always do the same thing
and this year I said I wasn't going. But my
parents insisted because they said it would
look rude. I wouldn't have minded if it was
just the afternoon but I wasn't looking
forward to the whole day. When I got there
though my cousin had brought a couple
of her friends and we sat together. I had a
good time but I would still have preferred to
stay at home.

Announcer: Speaker 2

Teenage boy: Every year someone in my family arranges
a day out in London for all of us. This year
my mum and I did it and we chose to go to
a musical. It was difficult to find a show that
would appeal to everyone and we were a
bit worried that my granny or my cousins
wouldn't like it, as in my family everyone
says what they think. So when everyone
said they'd had a great time, we knew we'd
made the right choice. Nobody complained,
even when we missed the train home and
we had to wait an hour in the station.

Announcer: Speaker 3

Teenage girl: Last weekend my aunt and uncle and
cousins were staying and we decided to
go out for the day. We were going to the
seaside but we hadn't gone far when we
drove past the zoo and my cousins said they
wanted to go in. So we decided we'd

---

go in for an hour and then carry on to the seaside. But there was so much to see that we stayed there all day. My mum and dad and my granny really aren't keen on zoos and were looking forward to a day on the beach but the rest of us didn't mind at all.

Announcer: Speaker 4

Teenage boy: My sister's birthday is in the summer so we usually go out somewhere for the day. She said she wanted to go to a theme park this year which was good for me as I don't usually want to do what she suggests. It's a new park quite near where I live. I only went on half the rides I wanted to because it's huge. The whole park shut at six – I suppose because it was getting dark. It didn't matter though because mum and dad said we can go again. They enjoyed sitting in the café and reading the newspapers.

Announcer: Speaker 5

Teenage girl: Last Sunday I went to the seaside with my family. My brother and sister are older than me and they didn't really want to come but I persuaded them as otherwise it would have been a bit boring with mum, dad and my grandparents. When we got there, we had a swim in the sea and a lovely picnic which my granny made. We agreed that we'd take a boat out in the afternoon but when we went to get one they were all out, which was a real shame. Unfortunately we hadn't realised we needed to book. So we just went for another swim and then came home.

Reading Part 3

1D 2B 3C 4B 5A 6D 7E 8A 9E 10C 11B 12A
13C 14E 15B

Unit 2

Grammar

❶ careful, more careful, carefully; easy, easier, easily; healthy, healthier, healthily; fast, faster, fast; good, better, well; terrible, more terrible, terribly; successful, more successful, successfully

❷ 2 successful   3 carefully   4 easier
    5 well   6 terribly   7 better   8 careful

❸ 3 Tennis is the more hardest sport to learn.
    5 It's less easier *easy* to learn a new sport as you get older.
    6 For me, playing computer games is the more *most* relaxing way to spend my free time.
    7 Joining a sports club can help people to become more healthier.
    8 I am the fittest now than *that* I have ever been in my life./I am the fittest *fitter* now than I have ever been.

Writing

A: Sentences 6 and 8;   **B:** Sentences 4 and 7;
C: Sentences 3 and 9;   **D:** Sentences 1 and 2

Vocabulary

❶ ⓐ
    1 amazing   2 thrilled   3 worried   4 embarrassing
    5 disappointed

ⓑ
    1 astonishing   2 delighted, pleased
    3 concerned, irritated   4 awkward, sad, upsetting
    5 upset, frustrated

❷ 2 E   3 C   4 B   5 A   6 D

❸ 2   shot off
    3   set off
    4   cut off
    5   let me off
    6   put off

❹ **take up**: an idea, a sport
    start up: a business, a machine
    make up: a story, an excuse

Listening Part 4

1B   2B   3A   4A   5C   6B   7A

Recording script   CD1 Track 3

Interviewer: So Toby how did you get into playing chess?

Toby: Well, I started playing with my dad when I was about 11 and I joined my club four years ago when my mom found an article in a local newspaper about the team from our local chess club winning a national tournament. My mom thought I would learn a lot from these guys. Now I'm one of the best players. All my opponents are much older than me but I'm used to it because it's like that everywhere. Anyway there are not too many players my age.

Interviewer: Playing chess on the internet is very popular now, isn't it? Would you recommend that to new players?

Toby: I used to play chess on the internet a lot and it was good up to a point. But I don't anymore because I found my game wasn't developing. Anyway, there's nothing like the thrill of playing face-to-face. It's more exciting and more challenging.

Interviewer: Has watching the grand masters play helped to develop your game?

Toby: Oh definitely. Veselin Topalov is my favourite player. He's an aggressive player and risks everything to win, and he doesn't mind sacrificing pieces if he has to. Sometimes I think he's going to lose and then I'm really surprised when he wins.

Interviewer: So what's the secret of your success? How do you decide which moves to make?

Toby: When making a move, I normally go on intuition. I'll look at the position and say, 'Which move looks comfortable to me?' After that, I choose about three moves and analyse them. I play some variations in my head. What would the position be after three moves or five moves? I look at the plans of the opponent to see if I have to do something against them or not. There is no best way to play a position. It depends on the player. But most of the time, it's just a question of knowing when to make an aggressive move and when to play a defensive move. It comes with experience.

Interviewer: Do you think you'll ever get to be a grand master yourself?

Toby: At the moment my ambition is to be ranked inside the top 100 players younger than 21 in the US Chess Federation. I'm currently ranked in the top 150 but I don't see my future career in chess.

Interviewer: Why's that?

Toby: Well, for one thing, I don't think I have the personality you need to be one of the top players. I probably could, if I really put a lot of effort into it, be a chess trainer but it doesn't pay well. So it's better for me to play for fun.

Interviewer: Experts always recommend that parents teach their children chess to help them learn about logic. Do you think that's useful?

Toby: Yes. I think chess can teach you a lot of things. You learn how to read a person by analysing the way they play chess. You find out what kind of person they are; whether they're creative or analytical. For example, some people's body language also helps you to see if they are confident or worried but the best players are very controlled.

Interviewer: Some people say that a game of chess is like the game of life. Do you agree with that?

Toby: No, I don't think chess is like life. I mean in some ways I suppose you could say it's similar. Many people set themselves targets and plan ahead for the future, for example. But in my mind, it's really important to separate chess and life because in chess, you can plan every move you make and you have a fairly good idea of what will happen next. And that's not true in life.

Interviewer: OK, we'll take a break now and ... *(fade)*

Use of English Part 4

1 found the race really exciting
2 was not/wasn't as expensive as
3 was disappointing for
4 was what Lucy enjoyed
5 because she took
6 like hockey as much
7 is the least exciting/interesting
8 such a confident player

Use of English Part 2

1 They   2 who/that   3 in   4 if/when   5 It/This
6 there   7 Each/Every/The   8 going/likely
9 be   10 and   11 Your   12 why

Unit 3

Grammar

① 2 was still looking; stopped   3 met; were going
4 sat; didn't eat; talked   5 woke up; were travelling
6 crossed; began   7 reached; knew   8 arrived;
weren't waiting; took

② 2 had been trying   3 had owned   4 had been feeling
5 'd/had forgotten   6 'd/had been standing up

③ 2 had ever been skiing   3 had been looking
4 were driving   5 started   6 got   7 wasn't   8 said
9 went   10 got   11 looked   12 had been snowing

❹ 2 My father's family used to own a cottage by the sea. The last time we went there I was 16.

3 In the 1950s, most people used to travel by bus and train but this soon changed as car ownership grew.

4 That's the house where I used to live before we moved to the city.

5 Nicholas didn't use to go to the gym so often when he had to commute.

6 The library used to be much busier before everyone had the internet.

Vocabulary

❶ 2 poisonous **3** scientific **4** salty **5** successful **6** energetic **7** dramatic **8** friendly **9** sympathetic **10** thoughtless

❷ Across: 2 activity **5** cruise **8** journey **9** voyage **10** flight
Down: 1 way **3** trip **4** ferry **6** hostel **7** travel

Reading Part 1

1B **2**C **3**D **4**A **5**A **6**C **7**B **8**D

Listening Part 1

1B **2**C **3**C

Recording script CD1 Track 4

Announcer: One. You overhear someone talking to a tour guide. Why is she talking to him?
  A to make a complaint
  B to make a suggestion
  C to ask for advice

Tourist: I just wanted to say, yesterday evening, when we went round the town, sightseeing, it was really good to have you show us everything and tell us where to go and what to do. I know later in the week we're going on another tour which is in the afternoon this time. So it'll be hot and I think it would be a good idea to have a break and get a drink in a café in the middle of the tour. It was OK yesterday because it was evening but I don't think I can manage to walk round for two hours in the heat.

Announcer: Two. You hear a man talking on the radio about a place he visited on holiday. What does he recommend?
  A the countryside
  B the entertainment
  C the shops

Male: It's not yet been discovered by most tourists so don't bother going there if you're looking for nightlife. You will though want to have space in your suitcases to bring home some of the local crafts and you can spend hours wandering the streets going in and out of the shops spending your money. Apart from that, there's not really much else to do. You can get a bus into the surrounding countryside but, to be honest, it's a bit dull. You'll have to entertain yourself by sitting in a café and watching people. That always fascinates me –
other people's lives are more interesting than mine!

Announcer: Three. You overhear two people talking about a holiday. What went wrong?
  A The hotel was full.
  B The suitcases got lost.
  C The plane was delayed.

Male: Well, the holiday could have been better.

Female: Oh, it wasn't that bad. I mean, when I realised our flight was three hours late arriving I thought 'Oh no, that's when the bags get on the wrong plane and in the wrong place'.

Male: I know. I was worried too. I hate not having all my things.

Female: But we were lucky there.

Male: Not so lucky with the hotel though.

Female: Our room was OK.

Male: Well, I'm not surprised it wasn't fully-booked even at the busiest time of year. I won't go back there again.

Unit 4

Grammar

❶ 1B **2**B **3**A **4**B **5**C **6**B **7**B **8**A **9**A **10**C

❷ 3 The problem is children generally eat too ~~little~~ *few* vegetables.

5 It's been such *a* long time since I've had fresh strawberries.

7 There's so ~~many~~ *much* salt in this that I can't eat it.

8 The restaurant wasn't ~~so~~ *as* good as I had expected.

9 He can cook much ~~more~~ better than I can.

10 There ~~isn't~~ *aren't* enough tomatoes for the salad.

Vocabulary

❶

burnt	fresh	mild	mouldy	raw	ripe
all	all	cheese	bread cheese	meat fish vegetables eggs fruit	vegetables cheese fruit

rotten	sour	stale	strong	tender	tough
meat fish vegetables cheese eggs fruit	milk	bread	cheese	meat vegetables	meat

❷ 1 tough   2 sour   3 ripe   4 rotten   5 fresh   6 stale
7 mouldy   8 mild, strong   9 Raw   10 tender   11 burnt

Sentences with a negative meaning: **1, 2, 3, 4, 7, 11**

❸ pineapple, strawberry, melon, nectarine, plum, cherry, pear, grape, apple, raspberry

N	B	A	N	A	N	M	R	G	Y
E	M	A	N	P	P	L	U	M	R
C	O	C	M	P	O	M	P	L	A
T	L	L	E	L	O	G	E	I	S
A	P	L	L	E	R	R	A	M	P
R	A	F	O	B	D	A	R	P	B
I	P	I	N	E	A	P	P	L	E
N	S	E	P	A	R	G	A	R	R
E	Y	Y	R	R	E	H	C	O	R
S	T	R	A	W	B	E	R	R	Y

Writing

1E   2C   3A   4D   5B

Listening Part 2

1 responsibility   2 perfection   3 team   4 ingredients
5 celebration   6 detail   7 seasonal
8 September   9 review   10 500

Recording script   CD1 Track 5

Interviewer: Thanks for agreeing to see me today, Ivor. I know you're very busy.

Ivor: That's all right. It's a pleasure.

Interviewer: I'm doing an article for my magazine and first I'd like to know what you enjoy about running your restaurants.

Ivor: Mmm. Well, what I find immensely satisfying and exhausting at the same time is the huge responsibility. It can be quite frightening, though, at times.

Interviewer: Yes, I can imagine. Why do you think your restaurants are so popular?

Ivor: We do get a lot of repeat business, you know, customers come back to us again and again. What they're looking for is a level of perfection that's not easy to find in most restaurants. In fact it's not easy for us to achieve day in and day out. But that's what separates us from the crowd, I think.

Interviewer: What advice would you give to someone starting a restaurant?

Ivor: I think it's essential to build a strong team. Without that the business can't succeed. We're like a family. Everyone has to play their part.

Interviewer: How do you train your staff?

Ivor: Well, the first thing I train them to do before they try and make a dish is to work out what the ingredients are. That's the starting point. How can they cook something if they can't taste what's in it?

Interviewer: What's the worst problem you've had to deal with?

Ivor: Well, we had one restaurant a few years ago that wasn't doing very well. It was full at the weekends but empty during the week. People were only booking it for a celebration of some kind. So we made a few changes, made it more relaxed so people felt it was somewhere they could go every day of the week.

Interviewer: You mentioned this earlier but can you explain in a bit more detail why you think your customers are so loyal?

Ivor: The key is to be consistent. You can't provide an excellent service one day and then not deliver the next. We have to make sure that every customer receives the same level of service. And I think it's the commitment to detail that keeps our standards so high.

Interviewer: Right. So how do you choose what goes on the menu?

Ivor: Well, that's what's so wonderful about cooking; it's seasonal, so the kind of things we cook changes every three months or so. In summer it's really light and fresh with lots of fish and salads. Then after that the food starts to get richer and heavier in September. There's more red meat and game on the menu for example.

Interviewer: How do you manage to keep your staff motivated all the time?

Ivor: That's an interesting question. When they've done a good job, I tell them but one thing I don't do is to let them see every fantastic review we get. I'm more interested in finding out what we can do better and how we can continue to learn.

Interviewer: Do you ever get any complaints?

Ivor: Hardly ever about the food. Sometimes people aren't happy because they can't get a table. We get over 500 calls a day for Novello's, where there are just 20 tables. That's about 3,000 calls a week! Demand is really high and we have to make sure that people aren't disappointed.

Use of English Part 4

1 rather than go/going   2 had already eaten enough
3 told us/me to try/told me about   4 weren't as strong as
5 not any fish left/no fish left   6 advised me to have/
advised having   7 were too few   8 didn't have much

Use of English Part 3

1 successful   2 conclusion   3 variety   4 freshness
5 envious   6 uninspired/uninspiring   7 significant
8 international   9 recognition   10 biggest

Unit 5

Grammar

❶ 2 wore   3 helps   4 don't make   5 want   6 are
   7 had   8 need   9 would come   10 'll/will see

❷ 2 if there are any coach trips?
   3 how much they cost?
   4 where they go?
   5 if I should put my name on a list?

Vocabulary

❶ 2 attend → expect   3 assist → attend
   4 know → find out   5 take part in → join
   6 know → get to know   7 took part in → attended
   8 attend → see

❷ 1 term   2 course   3 assignments   4 research
   5 tutor   6 tutorials   7 marks   8 degree

A	T	W	Q	U	T	Y	R	E	C	B
H	S	X	T	E	A	R	U	T	S	M
G	O	S	I	E	S	T	G	A	L	I
W	R	N	I	R	O	T	U	T	A	U
G	E	I	M	G	H	K	U	Y	I	K
X	S	R	A	E	N	M	R	T	R	U
I	E	A	B	D	W	M	E	E	O	R
T	A	C	O	U	R	S	E	A	T	M
E	R	F	V	R	B	N	I	N	U	Z
U	C	U	C	K	V	E	E	L	T	I
P	H	Y	L	A	J	M	A	R	K	S

❸

-ation	-ence	-ment	-ance
cancellation	dependence	development	performance
imagination	existence	arrangement	disturbance
preparation	difference		insurance

1 cancellations   2 imagination   3 insurance
4 existence   5 disturbance

Reading Part 2

1C   2B   3D   4F   5G   6A   7H

Listening Part 1

1B   2A   3C

Dad: Why do you think that? You've always been fascinated by the landscape and how it was formed.

Girl: But it's much more than that. We have to spend so much time doing research and drawing graphs. It's all statistics.

Dad: But what about that trip you made to the south of France? You enjoyed that.

Girl: I know. But we were supposed to be looking at the cliffs and the beaches and I spent all my time in the museums. I realised I'm much more interested in the history of places.

Dad: Well, now you're half way through, I think you should stick with it.

Announcer: Two. You hear two students talking about their friend Amy. What do they decide to do?
A   talk to her
B   talk to her tutor
C   talk to her parents

Girl 1: I'm worried about Amy. She hasn't done any work this term.

Girl 2: I noticed that she's missed a lot of tutorials. Should we say something to her?

Girl 1: I think we should speak to her mum and dad.

Girl 2: Surely it's her tutor's responsibility?

Girl 1: It is I suppose. I'm in the same group for some things so I could ask her tutor to talk to her.

Girl 2: I think we should start with Amy herself. She's over there look – I'll have a word now.

Girl 1: Good. I'll come with you. Perhaps we can persuade her to talk to her tutor then her parents need never know.

Announcer: Three. You hear someone talking on the radio about studying abroad. What does he recommend?
A   spending up to six months
B   living with a family
C   socialising often

I studied at a university in Brazil recently. It was good to have a whole year. I think if you stay less than six months you haven't got time to get used to the way of life. Because I was studying fewer subjects than the Brazilian students I had more free time and I think that's really important because that's when you learn the language – you know, when you mix with people. So don't sign up for a course which keeps you in the library all day. I lived with a family but I met all my friends at the university.

If there's a choice, it's best to live with people of your own age.

Use of English Part 3

1 establishment   2 effective   3 inhabitants
4 knowledge   5 enjoyable   6 cookery/cooking
7 possibilities   8 location   9 requirements
10 recommendations

Unit 6

Grammar

❶ 2 is driving   3 I'll be having
4 We'll have avoided   5 will be becoming
6 will have prevented   7 are turning down
8 they are starting   9 I'm taking   10 will have been

❷ 2 won't be/'re not going to be   3 will have run out
4 'm not going/won't go; 'm going to cycle/I'll cycle
5 will give up/are going to give up   6 is going to be/
will be   7 will improve/is going to improve; will use
8 will be   9 will be/are going to be   10 won't be/isn't
going to be

Vocabulary

2 increased risk of disease   3 heat waves   4 flooding
5 drought   6 loss of biodiversity

Listening Part 3

1E   2D   3C   4A   5B

Recording script   CD1 Track 7

Announcer: Speaker 1

People won't stop driving because the "improvements" to the public transport network aren't adequate. Before planning a scheme like this, they need to make public transport much cheaper and more efficient. The scheme may be successful in reducing congestion but air quality won't improve because people will either find alternative routes or drive to places where they won't be charged for using their cars, and in many cases people will have no choice – they'll just have to pay the charge. It's just another way to take money off of us!

Announcer: Speaker 2

We can't go on as we are and our roads just get more and more congested each year. A journey to my local supermarket which used to take 5 minutes now always takes me at

---

least 15 minutes because of the traffic. While I appreciate it's going to make life more difficult for some people, something has to be done to reduce congestion and pollution. Most people won't be affected too badly so why is everyone against the idea of congestion charging?

Announcer: Speaker 3

It will affect us in lots of ways, none of them positive. Firstly, our costs will go up as our suppliers will charge us more for bringing goods into the city centre. Secondly, it will cost our employees more to get to work; for some of them who work at night, public transport isn't an option, so it may be harder for us to recruit staff. And thirdly, it will affect our customers because it will be more expensive and less convenient for them to get to us, which means they may go elsewhere.

Announcer: Speaker 4

The congestion charge will literally be a breath of fresh air to local residents. Not just because there'll be less traffic in the area and so less noise and pollution, but because we will all get a 90% discount on paying the congestion charge! Anyway, it really isn't necessary to have a car if you live here. We're so close to the centre of the city that it's not as though it's far to get the tube or bus to get to work or to go shopping.

Announcer: Speaker 5

I think it's the only way to persuade people not to use their cars. Surely the aim of discouraging people from driving into the city centre is a good thing? I'm sure once people realise there's less traffic on the road, they'll be more inclined to start cycling. It'll be much safer without all those big lorries thundering past. People may even get into the habit of walking again which will be much better for their health as well as for the environment.

Writing

❶ 1D 2E 3A 4B 5C

❷ 1 A, C 2 A, B, C 3 A, B 4 A, C
5 B, C 6 A, C

❸ **Sentence 1:** fantastic, wonderful, (an) excellent

Sentence 2: fantastic, wonderful, (an) excellent, useful, (an) effective, (an) efficient

Sentence 3: fantastic, wonderful, (an) excellent, (an) effective, (an) efficient

Use of English Part 2

1 being 2 These 3 which 4 whereas/while/but
5 are 6 with 7 Because 8 from 9 other
10 towards/to 11 but 12 against/from

Use of English Part 4

1 despite the depressing 2 unless we do more
3 are at risk from 4 haven't done enough
5 to avoid wasting time in 6 is/has been six months since 7 would always freeze over 8 had already left when/before

Unit 7
Grammar

❶ 2 equipment 3 food 4 bags 5 information
6 vacancies 7 suggestions 8 dish 9 luggage
10 experience

❷ 2 a 3 a 4 the 5 the 6 a 7 a 8 – 9 – 10 a
11 a 12 the 13 a 14 a 15 a 16 the 17 –

Writing
ⓐ

	Answer A	Answer B
Does the student mention their experience?	✓	✓
Does the student say they are good with people?	✓	✓
Does the student say when they can work?	✗	✓
Does the student say what they are doing now?	✗	✓
Does the student say why they are suitable for the job?	✓ but only mentions experience not personality	✓
Has the letter got a good beginning?	✓	✓
Has the letter got a good ending?	✗	✓

ⓑ Letter B is the best answer because it gives a variety of information and answers all the questions. It has a better ending.

C **A:** paragraph breaks after *Richardson,*; *Sports Shop*; *meeting new people*; *good worker*
B: paragraph breaks after *Richardson,*; *advertisement*; *life-guard*; *yours*; *references*; *from you*; *sincerely*

Vocabulary

3 occasions → opportunities   **4** ✓
5 an opportunity → a possibility/a chance
6 funny → fun   **7** ✓   **8** work → job   **9** ✓
10 occasion → opportunity/chance

Listening Part 1

1B   2A   3B

Recording script   CD1 Track 8

Announcer: One. You overhear two people talking at the end of the day. Where are they?
　　　　A   in a shop
　　　　B   in an office
　　　　C   at home

A: Oh, I'm ready to put my feet up on the sofa now. What a day!

B: I've had quite a good day but I am looking forward to watching TV tonight. I don't have any work to take home for once.

A: I've got loads to do but it'll wait till Monday.

B: I'll walk with you if you're ready. I need to stop at the supermarket though to get something for dinner.

A: Oh, could you get me some milk? I just need to send a couple of emails. I'll see you outside the supermarket entrance in five minutes.

Announcer: Two. You hear a man talking on the phone about a job he has been offered. How does he feel?
　　　　A   confused
　　　　B   relieved
　　　　C   surprised

Yeah, they've offered it to me. Well, as soon as I went into the interview I kind of knew I was right for the job so I was really expecting to be offered it. But now it's actually happened I've realised that I've got to move to Germany and I don't know anyone there. It's a good job of course so I should take it. In fact it's the job of my dreams but now I've also been offered one nearby. If I took that one, I wouldn't have to move but it's not so interesting.

Announcer: Three. You hear a woman talking on the radio about her job. What does she say about it?
　　　　A   It's tiring.
　　　　B   It's interesting.
　　　　C   It's exciting.

Well, my job is quite varied and I really enjoy it. I know there are some photography jobs which take you to all kinds of amazing places so some people would find my job a bit boring maybe, taking photos of children all day long. It's mainly children. Their parents bring them to the studio and sometimes I take family groups. But I love it and the day passes so fast because the whole process fascinates me – getting the right shot and every one is different. I'm on my feet nearly all day but I'm used to that so it doesn't bother me.

Reading Part 3

1C   2A   3B   4D   5C   6A   7A   8D   9B   10C   11C
12D   13B   14C   15A

Unit 8

Grammar

1

Correct sentences: 1a   1b   3b   4a   4b   5a
5b   6b

Corrected sentences:
2a There was no point windsurfing because there wasn't any wind.
2b There wasn't enough wind to continue windsurfing.
3a I regret not finishing the race.
6a It wasn't worth going on, the climb was too dangerous.

2a and 2b: in sentence a, the person hasn't started windsurfing   3a and 3b: in sentence a, the person is talking about one race; in sentence b, the person is talking about racing in general   5a and 5b: in sentence a, the person had a rest after running 5km; in sentence b the person rested before completing 5km and then didn't have any more rests during the run

Vocabulary

1 after   **2** on   **3** off   **4** up   **5** to

Writing

recomendations – recommendations
conviniently – conveniently
acommodation – accommodation
confortable – comfortable   excelent – excellent
bycycle – bicycle   wether – weather
oportunities – opportunities   wich – which
belive – believe

Listening Part 2

1 size   **2** explorer   **3** challenge   **4** darkness
5 problem-solving   **6** risks/a risk   **7** Getting lost
8 training   **9** panic   **10** confidence

Recording script   CD1 Track 9

Debbie: Cave diving, officially the world's most dangerous sport, isn't for everyone. If you're the kind of person who enjoys being underwater in dark, enclosed spaces then it's probably the ultimate adventure sport. But for the rest of us it sounds like our worst nightmare. Barry Helman, who's just written 'A cave divers guide to diving', is here to explain what attracts people to the sport. Welcome to the show, Barry. So, why *do* people go cave diving?

Barry: Thanks Debbie. Well, I guess there are a number of reasons. For me it's the amazing beauty of these caves, not to mention their incredible size. It's like nowhere else. You're looking at rock formations that are millions of years old and the water is crystal clear. Another thing I like is that I'm seeing things that no one has ever seen before; I'm like an explorer discovering new places. Of course, if you don't know what you're doing it can be very dangerous but that's what some divers say they love about it. They enjoy the challenge.

Debbie: Don't you ever get scared?

Barry: Well, as I said, if you know what you're doing then you shouldn't have a problem. I think the worst thing that can happen is if your lights go out for some reason; it can be pretty disorienting being in total darkness. So that's why it's important to take two sets of lights with you. The other thing is that you can't immediately escape to the surface if you get into difficulties, which means your survival depends on your problem-solving abilities. Having said all that, cave diving isn't dangerous if you follow a few simple rules. Most of the accidents you read about could have been avoided if these people had followed simple steps to minimise the risks involved. It's also very important to know when to 'call a dive', or go back. And this is the first important lesson to learn. Another big danger is getting lost. Imagine entering an underwater room and looking back to see there is not one, but dozens of passages, and not knowing which way leads back to the entrance. So it's obviously only a sport for experienced divers; and you should never attempt cave diving without adequate training.

Debbie: It sounds like it takes a special sort of person to become a good cave diver.

Barry: I think that's right. You must be the kind of person who doesn't panic if something goes wrong, and that takes a great deal of self-control. However, you can learn a lot about yourself from diving and I think knowing you can survive in such a demanding environment gives you greater confidence, both at work and socially.

Debbie: Thanks very much Barry. Well, as you can see there are lots of good reasons for taking up cave diving. Barry's new book is out on the 21st of April and …

Use of English Part 1

1B   **2**B   **3**A   **4**C   **5**A   **6**B   **7**D   **8**B   **9**A   **10**B
11D   **12**C

Use of English Part 2

1 of   **2** be/get   **3** have/need   **4** There   **5** able
6 which   **7** That/This/It   **8** in   **9** more/better   **10** for
11 your   **12** how

Unit 9

Grammar

❶ 2 My whole family watched it yesterday and we all liked it.
3 I've never seen it and I don't want to.
4 I'm going to watch it next week.
5 I can't wait for the next episode because I'm really enjoying it.
6 I've only seen one episode and it was a bit boring but I might watch it again.

② ⓐ

B warn C complain D promise E announce
F admit

ⓑ

2 the food tasted disgusting.
3 she would give the money back the next day.
4 he was going to live in Brazil.
5 the city centre could be dangerous at night.
6 she had told a lie.

Vocabulary

❶ Across: 4 public **5** acting **8** presenter **9** drama
10 cartoon **11** scene **13** producer **14** spectators
Down: 1 documentary **2** contestant **3** stage
4 performance **6** comedy **7** audience **8** play
12 news

❷

2G 3A 4C 5E 6B 7D

Reading Part 2

1F 2D 3H 4A 5B 6G 7C

Listening Part 3

1B 2D 3A 4F 5E

Recording script CD1 Track 10

Announcer: Speaker 1

Have you seen *Black Watch 3* yet? I really enjoyed the other *Black Watch* films and this one is just as funny. It's got the same actors in it as the others and they're really good as usual. The story continues from the last film – you know when they were on that desert island – but even if you hadn't seen that you'd still be able to follow what was happening. But I was just getting involved in the story when it suddenly finished. It's only half the length of the other two films. It started well but didn't get a chance to develop properly.

Announcer: Speaker 2

I'd read about *The Purple Rose* and it sounded really good. I hadn't heard of any of the actors but they should get a lot more parts now after their performances in this film. The only problem was that there were five or six different storylines which made it very difficult to follow. It's full of action which meant I couldn't take my eyes off the screen and there are some good comedy scenes but I wasn't sure half the time why something was

happening. It could have been shorter too and it wouldn't have lost anything.

Announcer: Speaker 3

A Beautiful Land is set in New Zealand and is based on a book of the same name. They'd obviously gone to a lot of trouble to make sure they followed the story and the locations in the book. There are lots of beautiful shots. It's about two people who emigrated there a hundred years ago so it's a love story really and the two main actors are really good. But there's not much else to it and, to be honest, I couldn't wait for it to finish. It could have been at least 30 minutes shorter. It really wouldn't have made much difference.

Announcer: Speaker 4

Stephen Chadley is my favourite director so I was looking forward to his new film *Out of the Blue*. He always chooses at least one unknown actor as one of the stars and he's never made a mistake before. So, despite being set in a wonderful location in southern Thailand and having a really good script and gripping storyline, I didn't think any of the actors did a very good job, even those who are quite well-known. There were some funny moments though and it's got a very good ending – not what you'd expect at all.

Announcer: Speaker 5

Jack Bradley and Manuel Gonzalez star in *A Long Ride*. They are apparently good friends in real life. That came across in the film which is about a trip on a motorbike across South America. They didn't have a script – they just filmed what happened and a lot of interesting things did happen! The acting was of a really high standard but they are both very good comic actors and it was a shame they didn't take advantage of that – it could have been quite funny but was actually rather depressing. It was quite long but because they're always moving on to a new location, it didn't seem to matter.

Unit 10

Grammar

❶ 2 She could/might/may be working too hard.
3 He might not/may not/can't (NB NOT *could not*) earn very much.
4 That must be very hard
5 That can't be her grandfather.
6 He must have made a lot of money.
7 They can't have had another argument.
8 We may/might/could have met before.
9 She can't have had a happy childhood.
10 She may/might/could have thought I'd be angry.

❷ 1 must   2 may   3 might   4 must   5 could

Writing

❶ Correct sentence order: **D B A F C E**

❷ ⓑ

a) ending 2 focuses the most on the writer's feelings, ending 3 is the most factual
b) ending 2 contains the most complex sentences and the greatest range of structures (past simple, past continuous, past perfect, past modal)
c) ending 1 repeats 'wanted' to emphasise the number of visitors the writer received
d) ending 1 jumps to the next day without giving any information about what happened after he rescued the boy
e) ending 3 describes what happened after the rescue but this information is unnecessary because it's a bit boring and doesn't add anything to the story
f) ending 1 and ending 2 both make an impact; ending 1 shows other people's reactions to the rescue and ending 2 describes the writer's reactions well

Vocabulary

❶

make	have	cause
progress	fun	confusion
peace	patience	chaos
an effort	a shock	offence
changes		unhappiness
a mistake		

NB make fun of somebody = to tease

❷ 2 thoughtful   3 creative   4 friendly
5 easy-going   6 responsible   7 solitary
8 adventurous

The vertical word is: *sociable*.

Listening Part 4

1B   2C   3C   4C   5A   6C   7B

Recording script   CD1 Track 11

Interviewer: My guest this morning is Professor Martin Jackson from the Weller Institute, who's been doing some research into scientific studies on happiness. Welcome to the programme.

Professor: Thank you.

Interviewer: Is happiness something that can really be measured scientifically?

Professor: Oh, very much so. It's something psychologists have been studying for decades. Worldwide surveys investigating political changes have given us a very clear picture of how satisfied people are with their lives in different countries, for example. And we've discovered that simply by asking people how happy they are, we get a measure of happiness that is as good as the economists' measure of poverty or growth. What's new is that, in the same way that economic performance is used to measure government success, we expect that within ten years, governments will be judged on how happy they have made us.

Interviewer: That's very interesting. So individual happiness can really have an impact on society?

Professor: Yes. Some studies have shown that happy people live longer than depressed people. The difference can be as much as nine years between the happiest and unhappiest groups, which is very significant if you consider that heavy smoking can reduce life expectancy by as much as six years, with the average being three years.

Interviewer: That is quite surprising. Do the studies show if people are getting happier?

Professor: Interestingly, happiness levels have remained stable in industrialised countries for the last fifty years, despite dramatic increases in the standard of living. So, being richer isn't making us happier, although being poor does make people unhappy. But once you have enough money for a home, food and education for your children, extra money doesn't affect happiness.

Interviewer: So it's true that money can't buy happiness?

Professor: Well, we think that what happens when people buy things they think will make them happy, whether that's a new car or a bar of chocolate, is that the happiness they get from these things doesn't last. And so they need to buy more to get another short burst of pleasure.

Interviewer: I see. So I suppose what really makes people happy are their relationships with others.

Professor: Yes. This is the most important key to happiness. And it's the quality of those relationships that counts. So having one or two close friends is just as beneficial for happiness as having a wide circle of family and friends. It's even been suggested that friendship can protect against illness.

Interviewer: Really? What about work? Is that important for happiness?

Professor: Indeed it is. We've always known that people need to feel valued at work in order to be happy, and it goes without saying that people will feel happier if they actually enjoy what they're doing. But what we're discovering now is that having targets, which develop our skills and abilities, so that we reach our full potential, is essential for our happiness.

Interviewer: I suppose that makes sense. So is there a magic formula for happiness? I mean, is there anything people can do to make themselves happy?

Professor: Well, this is something that psychologists are trying to find out. There are action points which include things like smiling more and being helpful to other people, but there's no hard evidence yet that these things significantly improve happiness. What we do know, however, is that the biggest barrier to happiness is envy. So if we can try not to judge ourselves against other people, we'd certainly be happier.

Interviewer: Well, that sounds like really sound advice. Thank you very much. And if you've got any questions for Professor Jackson ...

Use of English Part 3

1 psychological 2 combinations 3 Comparisons
4 preference 5 typically 6 response 7 surroundings
8 emphasise 9 behaviour 10 different

Use of English Part 2

1 has 2 at/into 3 to 4 on 5 there 6 when
7 be 8 or 9 one 10 was 11 of 12 with

Unit 11

Grammar

❶ 2 wasn't able to/couldn't 3 can 4 haven't been able to 5 was able to/could 6 Will you be able to
7 was able to 8 can/is usually able to

❷ 3 Tommy looks ~~as~~ his grandfather at the same age. *like*
7 Your hands are as cold ~~like~~ ice. *as*
8 We didn't talk about the important things ~~as~~ where we would live. *like* or *such as*
10 I'm working in Italy at the moment ~~like~~ a tour guide. *as*

Vocabulary

❶ 1 department store 2 shopping centre 3 boutique
4 market 5 post office 6 delicatessen

❷ 2 out 3 away 4 up 5 down 6 out of 7 up
8 back 9 without 10 off 11 up

Reading Part 2

1C 2H 3E 4B 5F 6A 7G

Listening Part 1

1B 2A 3C

Recording script   CD1 Track 12

Announcer: One. You hear a woman talking to her son. Why is she talking to him?

    A to refuse permission
    B to make a suggestion
    C to give a warning

I'm happy for you to go on holiday with your friends and I'm sure you'll have a good time. I know you need some pocket money though and it really isn't going to help you if I give you money every time you need it. You already have your allowance and I don't know where that's all gone. It would be a good idea for you to earn some money by getting a weekend job. You've got time to save up. Then you might be more careful with it when you've got more idea of the value. So it's up to you to make a decision now.

Announcer: Two. You overhear a teenager talking to a shop assistant. What does he want to do?

A get a refund
B try something on
C exchange something

I bought this jacket last week and I really like it. I didn't have time to try it on so I took it home with me and tried it on there but it's too small.

I'm afraid I'll have to ask you for my money back. There isn't anything else here that I want at the moment or I could exchange it for something else. I could try a bigger one but they really look much too big and also they're not in the colour I want. I've got it here in the bag.

Announcer: Three. You overhear two people talking. Where are they?

A in a post office
B in a bookshop
C in a supermarket

Man: I've got to work here all weekend because it's going to be really busy apparently. I hope I get to stack the shelves rather than being on the till. People are in such a rush at the weekend.

Woman: Yeah, and some people just come in for a newspaper and they have to stand in a long queue. They get really annoyed.

Man: In my old job I used to be able to read a book when there were no customers.

Woman: There's no chance of that here!

Unit 12

Grammar

❶ ⓐ 1 who   2 which   3 where   4 which
5 whose   6 which   7 which   8 who
9 which   10 where

ⓑ 3 At my school, where there are many children from refugee families, they need to do more to get girls interested in sport.   5 The government, whose job it is to promote healthy eating, is not doing enough to encourage parents to change their shopping and cooking habits.   7 Childhood obesity, which is now a huge problem in Europe, may have a significant impact on life expectancy.

ⓒ 1, 2, 4, 6, 8, 9

ⓓ Relative pronouns can be omitted from sentences 4 and 9.

❷ 1D   2F   3A   4C   5B   6E

Writing

❷ 1F   2C   3H   4B   5G   6E   7A

Vocabulary

❶

C	H	E	A	N	K	L	E	X	C
E	L	B	O	W	N	O	Y	R	H
Y	E	R	T	E	E	U	E	O	I
T	K	N	C	H	E	S	T	C	N
H	E	E	L	W	R	I	S	H	T
I	B	S	H	O	U	L	D	E	R
G	T	O	I	N	G	O	N	E	L
H	H	O	P	N	T	O	E	K	I
M	U	F	D	E	W	R	I	S	T
C	M	O	P	C	H	E	S	H	P
O	B	A	C	K	I	Y	O	E	I
M	E	F	O	R	E	H	E	A	D

❷ ⓐ satisfaction   respect   capability   patience obedience   ability   pleasure   security

ⓑ

dis	im	in
dissatisfaction	impossibility	incapability
disrespect	impatience	inability
disobedience		insecurity
disability		
displeasure		

Listening Part 4

1C   2B   3B   4C   5A   6C   7B

Recording script   CD1 Track 13

Jake: Thank you for seeing me Doctor Reid. I've got some questions I need to investigate for my project on the effect of sleep on school students.

Dr Reid: OK. Well, perhaps we can start with your questions then.

Jake:	Well, the first thing I'm not sure about is whether people in general are sleeping less than in the past. I've read some reports on the internet which give conflicting information.
Dr Reid:	It's good to see you are checking your facts, the internet can be unreliable. As you know, today the average person gets about seven and a half hours sleep every night, which is a bit less than the recommended eight hours. However, without the interference of electric light bulbs and alarm clocks people usually sleep for nine hours and this was the case up to the early part of the 20th century.
Jake:	I thought so. And is it natural for people to just sleep at night like most people do now?
Dr Reid:	The sleep patterns we have developed are for the convenience of the working day not to suit our body clocks. Most people have a tendency to feel sleepy after lunch but because of the way our days are structured, most of us just have a cup of coffee and carry on, when we should let ourselves have a short sleep. But a constant need to nap is a sign that people aren't getting enough sleep at night, which is a problem that seems to be getting worse.
Jake:	I've read that it's a problem that affects teenagers in particular.
Dr Reid:	That's correct. A lot of teenagers are getting far too little sleep and there are concerns that this could have a serious long-term impact on their health but we don't know for sure yet. Researchers are also looking into how far a lack of sleep affects young people with depression. But one study has clearly demonstrated that high school students getting low grades also get on average one hour less sleep than students getting As and Bs.
Jake:	Really? Why do you think teenagers aren't getting enough sleep?
Dr Reid:	It's an interesting question. It's a problem that seems to affect all teenagers, not just the ones who eat the wrong things and who don't take any exercise. So my feeling is that parents need to take more responsibility. Too many teenagers watch TV in their rooms or play computer games until very late or they're allowed to go out on school nights.
Jake:	Some of my friends say they stay up late because they can't get to sleep if they go to bed earlier.
Dr Reid:	Well, there are things you can do to make yourself feel sleepy. Your brain needs to switch off and relax so don't have any drinks that contain caffeine, which includes hot chocolate and a lot of soft drinks. Reading a book you know well or listening to a story, rather than music, should help your brain to relax.
Jake:	So you shouldn't do your homework just before going to sleep?
Dr Reid:	Definitely not! Schools should be careful how much homework they set because working late in the evening doesn't help people to get a good night's sleep. It would be better for schools to stay open for longer so that pupils can do their homework before they get home to avoid this problem. Another thing that some schools have tried successfully is to begin the school day half an hour later, which seems like a good idea to me.
Jake:	Well, that's very interesting, thank you Doctor Reid. Just one last question. Is it true that our brains are actively thinking while we're asleep?
Dr Reid:	Well, our brains are good at sorting information while we are asleep. It's often the case that we wake up having found the answer to a problem that we'd been worrying about the day before. But it's important to write it down immediately as we can forget it easily.
Jake:	Great. That's all the information I need. Thanks very much for your help.

Use of English Part 4

1 advised me to give up   2 if you don't stop   3 whose children are overweight   4 suggested going/that we go   5 must have eaten more vegetables   6 playing tennis when I was   7 told Amy he would   8 was too tired to

Unit 13

Grammar

❶ 2 had started, would have driven   3 would have caught, had run   4 would have sat down, had been   5 hadn't felt, wouldn't have chatted   6 hadn't caught, wouldn't have met

❷ 2 hope   3 wish   4 hope   5 hope   6 wish   7 wish   8 hope   9 wish   10 wish

❸ 2b I wish the elephants ~~had~~ come closer.   *would*
4b If we ~~had~~ made a lot of noise, we would have seen more animals.   *hadn't*

Vocabulary

2 call   **3** called *or* named   **4** called   **5** called
6 called *or* named

Writing

1 B or C   **2** D or E   **3** B or C   **4** D or E   **5** B

Suggested answers
1 3A   **2** 5B   **3** 2E   **4** 4D   **5** 1C

Reading Part 1

1B   **2**C   **3**A   **4**B   **5**D   **6**B   **7**A   **8**D

Listening Part 2

1 a degree   **2** contact   **3** public speaking   **4** routine(s)
5 a boat/boats   **6** smell (of fish)   **7** negative
8 communicate   **9** films   **10** 14/fourteen

Recording script   CD1 Track 14

Presenter: In our series on different careers, today we are going to talk to Kirsty Willis who works in a zoo. Kirsty, welcome.

Kirsty: Thank you.

Presenter: So you're going to tell us what it's like working in a zoo.

Kirsty: Yes I am but there are also other careers with animals and I'm going to give some information about a few of them.

Presenter: Good.

Kirsty: OK. The job that most people associate with working with animals is in a zoo. Although there are job openings which don't require many qualifications, for most posts there's a lot of competition so it's unlikely that you'll be considered without a degree. Zoos have changed a lot over the years and focus on a conservation role nowadays which involves care, education and study. But don't expect to have very much contact with the animals because they tend to be left as much as possible to live as they would in the wild. Although you still may help with normal tasks of feeding, keeping records, etc., a lot of the time is spent on education so, you should have excellent public speaking skills. You will be talking to visitors to the zoo and showing groups of schoolchildren round and you need

to be able to get your enthusiasm across to them.

Because what happens in a zoo is more or less the same each day, the job will appeal to you if you like to have routines in your life. Another related area is working in aquariums with sea mammals and fish. You need similar skills to those required for working in a zoo but you also need to be able to swim well and have experience of using a boat as most of the aquariums have large areas of water. You will spend a large part of the day preparing and distributing the fishy diets, and dealing with chemicals that are used in the tanks. By the time you go home, you will almost certainly smell. It will be obvious to everyone that you've been working with fish!

Another job that immediately springs to mind when we mention working with animals is working as a vet. Training for this takes a long time, as long or even longer than for a doctor. You can work with all kinds of animals but you have to take into consideration that it can be frustrating because the animals can be very negative towards the vet. Conditioning tells them that every time this guy comes around, they aren't feeling well or it's going to be an uncomfortable, scary experience. To be a good vet, you don't just need knowledge of the science, you should be able to communicate with both animals and humans. That skill is really important.

The last job I'm going to talk about is being an animal trainer. These positions are generally in circuses and films. The training required to get there is primarily experience. The pay for these jobs can be pretty low and many people will work for free at first. It's also very hard work. The day starts early, as early as four or five in the morning and in most cases will not finish till fourteen hours later. Don't forget in most jobs you work eight hours a day maximum. This is definitely not a nine to five job!

There are other jobs of course like research or working for the government but I don't think we've got time to go into those here.

Presenter: That was absolutely fascinating, Kirsty, and I'm sure our listeners will feel the same. In the next programme, we …

Unit 14

Grammar

❶ ⓐ
2 She wants to have the windows cleaned.
3 She is going to have the hedge cut.
4 She would like to have the rubbish removed.
5 She thinks she should have the gate replaced.

ⓑ
7 She has had the windows cleaned.
8 She has had the hedge cut.
9 She has had the rubbish removed.
10 She has had the gate replaced.

❷ 2 I needn't have bought   3 wouldn't let me have
4 don't have to   5 can't   6 shouldn't have
7 were supposed to   8 Don't let the children
9 must   10 are allowed to

Vocabulary

2 likeable   3 traffic   4 gives an overview of
5 convenient   6 richly   7 poor   8 well-equipped

Listening Part 4

1B   2B   3C   4A   5C   6A   7B

Recording script   CD1 Track 15

Matt: Hello and welcome to the programme. This morning we're going to discuss 'kidults'; adults that stay at home with their parents until they're in their mid-twenties or even their mid-thirties. And here to tell us about the results of a recent survey on this subject is Sadie Andrews.

Sadie: Thanks Matt. Yes. Well the results show that the number of 18–24 year olds in Europe still living at home has reached 67%, although that figure is much lower for countries in northern Europe – Sweden has overtaken the UK and France as the country with the fewest 'kidults' with only 46% of this age-group still living at home. As you might expect, that figure rises to over 90% for countries in Southern Europe such as Spain and Italy, where young people have traditionally lived with their parents for longer. Despite lower unemployment and relatively low rents, there's little change here because family relationships remain very strong.

Matt: That's very interesting. And what about outside Europe?

Sadie: Yes. The survey also covered the United States where the trend is also for people to live at home longer, though here the reason given wasn't to do with people having to pay back huge student loans, as this is nothing new. 'Kidults' here said there was no reason for them to leave home because they got on so well with their parents. Many people reported continuing to live at home even after they got married. So there's obviously less of a generation gap than there used to be.

Matt: I can see there are advantages. Having your mum to do your washing and ironing, for example.

Sadie: People interviewed for the survey didn't admit to that – even if it were true – though I know my mum wouldn't be prepared to do my washing and ironing. In fact the impression I get is that the kidults are pretty responsible people. What they seem to appreciate most is having the opportunity to save the money they would otherwise spend on rent so they can eventually buy their own home, which seems like a good idea.

But of course, there are disadvantages. Interviewees report that having to tell their parents what time they'll be home or not being able to spend time at home with friends without first asking permission is a frustrating experience and they complain that a lot of parents still think of 'kidults' as just kids.

Matt: Yes. That must be difficult. What about the parents? What do they think?

Sadie: On the whole most don't seem to mind and are willing to help their adult children out wherever possible. However, in some cases parents find that just when they've reached the point in their lives when they have the time and the money to do whatever they want, they are held back because of their children's needs. On the other hand, there is evidence to show that having the kidults at home does prevent some marriages from breaking down. This often happens apparently; when a couple do get to spend time alone after raising a family, they find they have nothing in common anymore.

Matt: That's sad. So before we hear from the listeners, what advice would you give for families in this situation?

| Sadie: | Well, obviously things are going to run more smoothly if everyone involved does their fair share, so it's a good idea to work out a fair contribution for bills and jobs such as shopping and washing-up. However, feedback from the results from the survey suggests that deciding in advance how often they are going to eat together, if at all, and at what time, will avoid resentment building up on both sides. This causes more arguments than any other issue. |
| Matt: | Thanks Sadie. Right, if you've got any comments to make, please call … |

Writing

❶ 1F 2E 3B 4A 5C 6D

❷ 1, 2, 4

Use of English Part 1

1B 2C 3A 4A 5D 6C 7A 8C 9B 10D
11A 12B

Unit 15

Grammar

❶ 2 is organised 3 is given 4 has been raised
5 were awarded 6 was chosen 7 is hoped 8 will be offered/are offered 9 was formed 10 be seen
11 are already being made/have already been made
12 to be added

❷ 2 It is thought that the new airport runway will probably be built next year. 3 It is reported that the new team has been selected. 4 Federer is considered to be the best tennis player ever. 5 This summer is reported to be the hottest for 50 years. 6 It is believed that the bones found on a beach belonged to a dinosaur.

Writing

❶

Say which and why	Yes, explain	No, because	Suggest
D, G	H	C, F	B, E

❷ **Possible answers**
Dear Beth
I am glad to give you some advice about your music festival.
If the weather is bad, people won't come if it's in the park or on the school field so it's better to be inside. It rained all day when we had our festival.

Our school is quite small and we wanted to make sure we had a big audience. The performers brought all their friends with them so that was good.
It's difficult to know how much food to have or what people will eat so it's not a good idea to provide it.
You need to have music people can dance to and some music that the students' parents will recognise too, so a mixture is best.
I hope your festival is successful and that you will tell me all about it.
Best wishes

Dear Beth
I am glad to give you some advice about your music festival.
In summer, it's nice to be in the fresh air and also you will have more space for dancing so we preferred to be outside.
We decided we wanted a wide variety of music so we invited people of different ages to perform. You could ask the relatives of the students at your school.
You will probably need to sell drinks but it's very hard work to make food for everyone. You would need lots of people to help so I don't think it's a good idea to provide it.
The most successful performances were the bands which had young people in them. You could have a bit of classical music too though as some people enjoy that.
I hope your festival is successful and that you will tell me all about it.
Best wishes

Vocabulary

1 electrician politician <u>photographer</u> musician
2 <u>accountant</u> biologist scientist guitarist
3 fisherman/woman <u>cyclist</u> postman/woman policeman/woman
4 reporter designer manager <u>visitor</u>

Reading Part 3

1E 2A 3B 4D 5/6 A/C 7E 8C 9A 10B 11D
12B 13C 14E 15D

Listening Part 3

1B 2F 3D 4C 5A

Announcer: Speaker 1

We're going out later to celebrate my good news. Since I moved to a different part of the city it's really expensive getting to work and I don't earn much. So I've been looking for another job nearer to where I live. I had a couple of interviews last week but I wasn't that impressed, then today my boss said he was going to give me more responsibility and it will mean more money too. It's great because I don't feel so bad about having to pay for petrol now.

Announcer: Speaker 2

I called on Anita and she'd just arrived home with little Sam. He's beautiful and looks just like her. She wants us all to go round on Sunday to meet him properly and we can celebrate then. She needs a few days to recover from the birth first. And they only moved to that flat recently so she's been very busy what with the move and doing her last exams to become a lawyer. She hasn't got the results yet but I'm sure she did OK.

Announcer: Speaker 3

I just bumped into Olivia. She's finished her nursing course. She did really well and she's moving to London. She's going to work in a hospital as a midwife delivering babies. She only found out she got it today. She's so pleased as it's what she really wants to do and she'd like us to help her celebrate by going out for a meal tonight. She'll have to move to London of course, and it's really expensive to find a flat there but we'll be able to go and see her.

Announcer: Speaker 4

I've known George nearly all my life because his family lived in the flat next door to us till last year. We went to the same school and revised for our exams together but it was only last week that we decided to get married. He gave me this beautiful ring and we're having a party next weekend. The wedding will be in the summer and we're looking for a flat near the railway station because I need to catch the train to work and I don't want to have to change my job.

Announcer: Speaker 5

I decided to do another course rather than go for that job I applied for. It'll mean I can start off at a higher level if I have better qualifications. Anyway, I needed certain grades to get on the course and I got what I wanted! I got the results today so a few of us are going to have a party tonight to celebrate. Most people did well. Mark and I are thinking of getting engaged but we won't get married till after I've finished the course and I've found a job because we won't know where we want to live.

Unit 16

Grammar

❶ **2** in case   **3** If   **4** Even if   **5** whether   **6** in case   **7** when   **8** If   **9** even if   **10** Even though

❷ **2** asked/reminded/warned/told   **3** recommended/suggested   **4** accused   **5** offered/promised/agreed   **6** denied/admitted   **7** asked/reminded/warned/told/advised   **8** invited   **9** explained/admitted/denied/agreed **10** advised/warned/told/reminded

Writing

❶ **Yes:** 1, 2, 3, 4, 7, 9, 10
No: 5, 6, 8

❷ A great invention

There have been a lot of great inventions which have affected all our lives. Some of them, such as **(d)** the map, the ship and the gun/maps, ships and guns have completely changed history. However, I'd say the computer is the most amazing invention; even more important than **(d)** the car or the telephone/cars or telephones.

Nowadays we can't manage without computers, not only at work but also at home. I can't even imagine our world without this "clever machine".

(b) The computer plays **(e)** an essential role in office work because it can store **(c)** a huge amount/huge amounts of information. It can help you with your studies, correcting your grammar and training your language skills, for example.

But that's not all computers can do. I have found a lot of new friends thanks to the internet. You can also "travel" around the world using **(b)** the internet to find out what is happening in **(a)** different countries.

I believe that other uses for computers will be discovered in the future. Computers have changed people's lifestyles forever. And they will affect everyone's life directly or indirectly.

Vocabulary

Across: 1 virus **6** monitor **9** broadband **10** delete
Down: 2 incompatible **3** online **4** download
5 crash **7** database **8** cable

Listening Part 2

1 2025 **2** travel problems **3** payment(s) **4** TV programmes **5** diary **6** (the) fridge **7** map **8** wallet **9** memory **10** learn

Recording script CD1 Track 17

Interviewer: Now I expect like me you can't imagine life without your mobile phone. Even in a few short years they've changed beyond all recognition. But apparently this is only the start of things to come over the next two decades and here to tell us what we can expect is communications expert, Dr William West. Welcome to the programme. So how are mobile phones going to change?

Dr West: OK. You'll find that your mobile will be much more than just a communications device. By 2025 it will have become more like a remote control which you use to organise your everyday life. This is starting to happen now and our mobile phones are already doing things that were unimaginable even five years ago.

Interviewer: Can you give us some examples of what we'll use it for?

Dr West: Well, on a typical day, for example, it will start working even before you wake up. Because it knows your daily routine, it can check for travel problems and adjust the time it wakes you up accordingly, presenting you with your best route into work.

Interviewer: That'll be useful!

Dr West: Yes. And you won't need a credit card. Just by placing the phone near a sensor on a barrier, payment will automatically be made for tickets for journeys, or for items in shops.

Interviewer: That's incredible!

Dr West: You'll soon be taking it for granted, which is what happens with all good inventions. Something which I'm sure you'll like is being able to get your phone to find TV programmes which it knows will interest you, and then download them as a podcast for you to watch on the train while you're going to work. And when you get to work, your phone will intelligently work out what to do with incoming phone calls because it knows your diary. It'll automatically direct calls to voicemail when you're in a meeting for example.

Interviewer: So you think they'll make our lives easier?

Dr West: Oh yes. No question. We'll save a lot of time. You won't have to worry about what to cook in the evening because your phone will do that for you and come up with suggestions based on what it thinks will be in the fridge. It'll be able to work that out by using the shopping bill to calculate what's already been used from the weekly grocery shop.

Interviewer: Now that's what I call progress!

Dr West: You'll even be able to see where members of your family are on a map which shows their location.

Interviewer: I seem to remember Harry Potter having one of those!

Dr West: Yes, I think he did. It does all seem quite magical to us now but it won't be long before it's quite normal. And you won't dream of leaving the house without your phone just as you wouldn't go out without your wallet today.

Interviewer: I think that's already happened for quite a lot of people.

Dr West: Yes, you could be right there.

Interviewer: So how far off is this new technology?

Dr West: Actually not that far off. We already have widespread cellular coverage, and high speed data networks. What we need to do now is develop mobiles with much greater memory and intelligence. We've seen mobile phones develop from just being a device for making phone calls into a texting device, camera and music player. As software gets more sophisticated, it will also be possible for our phones to learn. This is only the start of an evolution that will turn them into our trusted and indispensable companion in life.

Interviewer: That's fascinating. Thank you so much for coming in today …

Use of English Part 3

1 considerable **2** strength **3** invention **4** weekly
5 impossible **6** technological **7** dramatic **8** scientific
9 choice **10** old-fashioned

Acknowledgements

The authors would like to thank Niki Donnelly for her management and guidance. Thanks also go to Sara Bennett and Judith Greet for editing the book.

Development of this publication has made use of the Cambridge International Corpus (CIC). The CIC is a computerised database of contemporary spoken and written English which currently stands at over one billion words. It includes British English, American English and other varieties of English. It also includes the Cambridge Learner Corpus, developed in collaboration with the University of Cambridge ESOL Examinations. Cambridge University Press has built up the CIC to provide evidence about language use that helps to produce better language teaching materials.

The authors and publishers acknowledge the following sources of copyright material and are grateful for the permissions granted. While every effort has been made, it has not always been possible to identify the sources of all the material used, or to trace all copyright holders. If any omissions are brought to our notice, we will be happy to include the appropriate acknowledgements on reprinting.

p. 7: Joanna Moorhead for the article 'Being an only child' The Guardian 4 March 2006. Reproduced by permission of Joanna Moorhead;

P. 10 and p. 70: Listening, part 4 and Recording Script 'Chess Isn't like life' by Tim Lytvinenko from Concord Monitor, 2 October 2006;

p. 14: James Whyte for the article 'In from the cold' The Guardian 25 March 2004. Copyright © James Whyte 2007;

p. 19: The Independent for the article 'Eating in Britain' from '50 Best Restaurants in the World' by Steve Bloomfield, The Independent 17 April 2005, and for the article on p. 38, 'I often spend the day shopping' from 'I want your job' by Alex McRae, The Independent 14 June 2007. Copyright © Independent News and Media Ltd;

p. 22: Article 'Studying Abroad' from www.kidshealth.org;

p. 27: UNEP/AEWA for the text 'The effect of climate change on migratory birds'. Copyright © WMBD. World Migratory Bird Day is an annual event initiated by the African-Eurasian Migratory Waterbird Agreement (UNEP/AEWA). www.worldmigratorybirdday.org;

p. 34: Smarter Travel Media LLC for the article 'Planning an Adventure Trip.' Some portions © 2006, Smarter Travel Media LLC. All Rights Reserved;

p. 35: Mountain Tracks for the article 'What is ski touring?' from www.mountaintracks.co.uk. Reproduced by permission of Mountain Tracks;

p. 42: BBC for the text 'Personality Types'. Reproduced by permission of the BBC. http://www.bbc.co.uk/science/humanbody;

p. 43: The Press Association for the article 'Happiest day of the year' by Antony Stone, published in The Independent 23 June 2006. Copyright © The Press Association;

p. 46: BBC News Online for the text 'Who's Playing Mind Games with you'? and for the listening exercise in Unit 16 'Future of Mobile phones' Reproduced by permission of BBC News at bbc.co.uk/news;

p. 54: Travel Africa for the text 'African Safari' from 'Undying teen appeal, it is a safari' by Martin Symington from http://www.travelafricamag.com. Reproduced by permission of Travel Africa Ltd;

p. 59: A L Kennedy for the article 'A Writer's Room' from http://books.guardian.co.uk. Reproduced by permission of A L Kennedy;

Key: l = Left, r = Right. t = Top, b = Bottom.

For permission to reproduce photographs: The Advertising Archives p. 67; Alamy/©Jon Arnold Images Ltd p. 12, /©Dan Burton p. 33 (r), /©Stuart Crump p. 55, /©Andreas von Einsiedel p. 58, /©JLImages p. 60, /©Mira p. 43, /©Miguel Angel Muñoz Pellicer p. 53, /©David Robertson p. 63 (tl), /©Alex Segre p. 47, /©Somos Images LLC p. 4, /©Jack Sullivan p. 15, /©Pete M. Wilson p. 62; Corbis/©Alexander Benz/zefa p. 7 (mr), /©Bernard Bisson/Sygma p. 31, /©Helen King p. 7 (bl), /©James Marshall p. 19, /©Roy Morsch p. 45, /©Anthony West p. 33 (l); Getty Images/AFP/Frederic J. Brown p. 63 (bl), /AFP/Patrick Lin p. 63 (br), /Aurora/PatitucciPhoto p. 35, /Daniel Berehulak p. 24, /Lonely Planet Images/Brent Winebrenner p. 26, /Stone/Daryl Balfour p. 54, /Stone/Emmanuel Faure p. 39, /Stone/Zubin Shroff p. 7 (tr), /Stone/Siri Stafford p. 7 (br), /Taxi/Phil Boorman p. 51, /Taxi/joSon p. 7 (tl), /Sion Touhig p. 63 (tr), /Wireimage/Richard Lewis p. 38; Guardian News and Media/©Jim Whyte 2004 p. 14, /©Eamonn McCabe p. 59; Lebrecht Music & Arts/©Jim Four p. 11; Rex Features/©Edward Hirst p. 28; VIEW Pictures/Edmund Sumner p. 18.

The publishers are grateful to the following contributors:

Judith Greet: editorial work

Ruth Carim: proofreader

Hilary Fletcher: picture research

John Green: audio producer (TEFL Tapes)

Tim Woolf: audio editor

Cover design and page layout: Wild Apple Design Ltd.

Audio recorded at: The Audio Workshop, London